The Rough Guide to

Children's Books

by
Nicholas Tucker

**ROUGH
GUIDES**

Contents

Introduction

C hoosing the right book for the right child is never a simple matter. *The Rough Guide to Children's Books 0–5* was written in the hope of making some of those choices easier. Over 140 of the very best children's books have been selected; written and illustrated by the most brilliant and distinctive children's authors and artists working today. Particular favourites from the recent past have also been included, plus a few older titles that now qualify as enduring classics.

The books have been ordered both by age and category: so, for example, Lucy Cousins' *Where Does Maisy Live?* appears in the 0–18 months section within the category Interactive Books, while Dr Seuss's *Green Eggs and Ham* appears in the 3½–5 section under Poetry. Each book is given a brief review explaining what it is about, before going on to discuss reasons for its appeal and its possible benefits for a young child. Suggested age-ranges are approximate, since some children are always likely to be further on in appreciating stories than others. Reviews usually concentrate on a single book, but whenever this is part of a series the other titles are indicated, and there are frequent suggestions for further reading. All selected titles were in print at the time of this book going to press.

Children within the 0–5 age group normally need to be read to. This is never just a matter of simply reading out each word on the page, since children often ask questions and make observations as a story goes along. They also hugely enjoy the warmth and intimacy of a reading session, and while audiotapes can be useful they lack the particular magic which a "live" reading or storytelling so often brings.

Small children can often be very destructive of their books – especially those they like most – but nowadays many books for the very young are produced in highly durable and user-friendly materials. Bookshelves can be difficult for young hands to pull books from, so keeping titles on horizontal surfaces may often be a better idea early on. While very beautiful or expensive books are perhaps best brought out only for special occasions, on the whole it is best to allow children instant access to a varied selection of books, letting them enjoy them in whatever way they like. That way, they can build up the kind of easy and intimate familiarity with books that can often lead to a lifetime of pleasure and enjoyment.

Acknowledgements

I would like to acknowledge the continuing help I have received from my many friends in the children's book publishing world. Unfailingly positive, conscientious, generous and open-minded, it is hard to imagine a nicer group of people, and I have much enjoyed and appreciated their company over the years. I would also thank my other friends with whom I have so often discussed children's books, in particular Nina Bawden, Geraldine Brennan, Joanna Carey, Nancy Chambers, Wendy Cooling, Julia Eccleshare, Penelope Farmer, Geoff Fox, Peter Hunt, Beryl McAlhone, Elaine Moss, Iona Opie, Philippa Perry, Chris Powling, Rick Rogers, Morag Styles, Victor Watson and Anne Wood. Extra special thanks here to Kim Reynolds, always up for new ideas as well as a constant source of stimulation herself.

At Rough Guides I would like to thank Mark Ellingham whose idea the books were, as well as Andrew Dickson, Helen Prior, and Joe Staines who has been a pleasure to work with from first to last. I would also like to thank my partner Kay Andrews for her kind encouragement. And finally, big thanks to Mimi Tucker for reminding me once again, and so delightfully, what it is like to be under two years old; this book is dedicated to her and to her yet unborn cousin with love.

Babies

Up to 18 months

Babies

Up to 18 months

Babies are born with limited vision, and it also takes them some time before they can control their head movements. But their enjoyment of sound and speech is there from the first moment, which is why singing, talking or reading to them has always proved both stimulating as well as potentially soothing. Lullabies, for example, are found in every country, simply because rocking babies to the steady rhythm of a song has always been an effective way of nursing them back to sleep.

Of course you don't need books to sing or talk to a child. But books do offer a useful structure for reading aloud to babies, particularly at times when your powers of verbal invention may otherwise be flagging. Parents often communicate with their infants using the same, few stock phrases. This is fine, given that babies never mind repetition at this early stage, but there is also room for some less predictable language of the type some-times found in books for the very young. Hearing new words, rhythms and rhymes read aloud over and over again is highly stimulating for babies. It will take them some time to recognize any accompanying pictures, but by ten months many babies are able to do this with familiar faces and objects as well as voices, and recog-nizing pictures in favourite books will soon follow. In the earliest stages of development, babies seem better able to cope with black and white rather than coloured pat-terns, and many modern baby books either cut down on colour or leave it out altogether. Brightly coloured books that also include simple, clearly defined shapes will become more popular once a child is past the first baby stages.

To survive the energetic attentions of infants, early books have to be sturdy as well as attractive. Publishers have always tried to meet this challenge, and recently board or cloth books for babies have improved out of all recognition. The toughened, laminated pages of board books too often went with inferior art and mechanical prose, but this is no longer the case, and some excel-lent artists and writers now cater specifically for this youngest of age groups. Should one particularly well-loved book eventually get battered almost out of recognition, this can also be a sign of how effectively it has done its job.

Early encounters with books can also be useful in that

they build up an expectation that reading with a parent is something that is nice to do. The physical contact involved, with babies sitting on laps and generally being hugged at the same time, is particularly valuable. But it is important never to force books on babies when they are restless and not in the mood. Making sure that you reach for a book when the time is right will help to foster an expectation of enjoyment that children can often associate with books and reading for the rest of their lives.

Upto 18 months

Play Books

There is a huge variety of play books available for babies, from traditional cloth books to modern innovations like the touch-and-feel range, or books that are actually designed to be taken into the bath. Some of these books could also be described as toys, but so long as they contain illustrations plus a few words then a baby can still get the feeling that here is something to look at and read with their parents. The best illustrators of these play books are skilled at suggesting objects and faces using just the minimum of detail that a baby is able to absorb. This ability to simplify complex objects in a way that also makes them immediately recognizable is also found in cartoon films, where cars, bicycles or whatever else are usually depicted stripped down to just a few salient details. Babies can be quite good at recognizing their own faces or those of people closest to them in photographs, but other objects or people less familiar to them can easily get lost in pictures where too much is going on and nothing is left out.

Choosing the best play books for any particular child is always going to be something of a leap in the dark, and sometimes the most unlikely books can prove firm favourites, but those mentioned below seem to me some of the best while also possessing a better track record than most when it comes to attracting and interesting the very young.

Around the Garden
Lucy Cousins (illustrator)
Walker Books (cloth)

Cloth books have been around for some time, but they often used to look very dreary. Advanced technology and a determination to raise standards have seen huge improvements in this area, with Walker Books leading the way with a series designed by Lucy Cousins. This is an excellent example of a hand-washable and non-fade wordless book, designed to introduce babies to common sights in the garden. Its contents include a bright red watering-can against a green background and on another page a beautiful pink butterfly. Other colours are also vivid and child-friendly throughout, with all four pages easy to turn over since they are bulked out with spongy material. Accompanying books in this series focus on the park, the farm and around

Upto 18 months

the house. With each page surrounded by green stitching and featuring a bright, child-like painting of a flower on the front, this book, like its companions, strikes a bright note even on the darkest of days.

Baby Faces
Sandra Lousada (photographer)
Campbell Books (board)

Baby Faces is made up of seven thick board discs loosely bound to each other by a cord that also threads through a noisy, green rattle on the outside. Each disc contains a black and white photograph of a real baby with a one-word description of his or her mood on the opposite side. There is a sad as well as a happy baby here, and a quiet as well as a noisy one. The final photo shows a baby waving goodbye. Babies themselves are often fascinated by other infants, and this offering in the Baby Campbell range could well hold some of the same interest for very young readers. The crying baby is particularly recognizable, but as all the other babies look so jolly, this "book" (if that is what it is) still comes over as a strongly positive experience for children still unaccustomed to thinking that there are plenty of other babies in the world apart from themselves.

Upto 18 months

8

Buggy Buddies: A Bear with a Pear
Nick Sharratt (illustrator)
Campbell Books (board)

This little book is threaded through by a bouncy plastic strap which can then be attached to the pram, buggy or whatever else babies may be parked in. It might seem a shame to deprive a baby of the endless pleasure of throwing everything out of the pram from time to

time, but most parents will probably be grateful for something that stays permanently inside. This particular book is small, brightly coloured and has thick, board pages that make turning over less difficult, although small babies will still take some time learning how to manage this simple skill. Nick Sharratt uses broad lines and a minimum of detail, and although this is a book about basic counting, it will be enjoyed more for its cheerful, primary colours and jolly rhymes ("A puffin with muffins; a poodle with noodles.")

Upto 18 months

Little Fluffy Mouse
Gerald Hawksley (illustrator)
Egmont Books (board)

This little board book has a continuous hole in the middle through which Fluffy Mouse, a toy attached to the middle of the last page, sticks his head in order to greet the reader. Every time a page is turned, this same Fluffy Mouse appears as the centrepiece to a new picture, each one illustrating his quest to find somewhere to live. Fed up with his house, Fluffy Mouse at the turn of a page imagines living in a tree, down a rabbit hole, in a pond with ducks or in a belfry with bats. At the final picture, with no more pages to turn, Fluffy Mouse agrees that perhaps the kitchen is the best place after all. It is then necessary to close the book and pull through Fluffy Mouse's head so that once again it sticks out in front. Children should enjoy the way that the mouse stays the same each time while the pictures around it change from page to page. Affectionately illustrated by Gerald Hawksley, this book is not recommended for children under twelve months in case the fur starts to shed. But a soft toy built into a board book is such a good idea that it is well worth waiting for, perhaps as a present on a first birthday.

The Rainbow Fish Bath Book
Marcus Pfister (author/illustrator)
North-South Books (cloth)

Adapted from a picture book, this soft book is perfect
for bath-time. Its pages are made from a sponge
covered in waterproof material, and a special type of
foil is stamped on each page to give the scales of the
rainbow fish hero their shining effect. Rainbow Fish is
gradually persuaded to share his scales with all the
other fish he knows, so that they all end up swimming
around in a glittering, happy ending. The pictures of
life at the bottom of the sea will look even more
authentic once they are plunged into the bath water,
but this charming and atmospheric little book is
equally effective on ground level and one of the best
bath books around.

Tiny Teethers: Zoo
Cathy Gale (illustrator)
Campbell Books (board)

This ingenious publication combines an easy-grip,
board book tethered by a plastic strap to a removable
water-filled teething ring. But that is all there is about
teething troubles, with pictures and a minimal text
focusing instead on animal activities on one page

Upto 18 months

complemented by a human baby doing much the same sort of thing on the other, each time chanting the same refrain: "And I can, too!" The actions include clapping, rolling on the back, splashing and jumping up and down. With each surface edge slightly curved inwards, this little book is as easy to grip as the teething ring itself – one more good idea in this consistently child-friendly series which includes the companion titles *Puppy*, *Farm* and *Teddy*.

Upto 18 months

Interactive Books

Joining in a story is something that comes naturally to small children, and this can make reading to them active and sometimes noisy – which is just as it should be, given that the essence of stimulating infants lies not so much in what adults say to them but in what they are encouraged to say in return. Later on such joining-in may follow more orderly patterns, such as repeating a favourite refrain contained in a story or poem. At an earlier stage, small children can be expected to try and make any animal noises contained in a story, and they may also soon be able to come up with the right answer when a story poses a particularly obvious question. Adult prompting will always help, particularly when infants are encouraged to make their own responses rather than having everything done for them.

There are of course many other ways of interacting with a book without involving speech at all. Touch-and-feel books, for example, help children develop a sensitivity to texture, and stories involving games of peek-a-boo may also stimulate a child's growing skills in being able to remember what was there even when the objects or people in front of them are temporarily hidden. Children learn through play – never more so than at this early age – and if an infant and parent develop a particular game around a favourite story, well and good. Not only will everyone be having fun, but there may also be some useful learning going on at the same time.

All Join In
Quentin Blake (author/illustrator)
Red Fox (pb)

This picture book is all about noise and reading it aloud is bound to lead to a noisy session in response, but this is such an infectiously joyful book it would be difficult to complain. A series of simple rhymes describe children making the various sorts of din they find enjoyable but which surrounding adults often complain about. Trumpets are blown, drum-kits are bashed and dustbins are kicked both in the verse and in Quentin Blake's accompanying illustrations. The faces of the middle-aged couple leaning out of their window, having been disturbed by a chorus of scrawny cats at the bottom of their garden, are wonderful studies in mute desperation. Various other adult victims of noise in these pages are equally memorable, and overall this is one of those picture books that is almost impossible to get through without smiling – however often it has been read before.

Fluffy Chick: Touch and Feel

Rod Campbell (illustrator)

Campbell Books (hb)

Touching and feeling are an essential part of the way in which babies explore the world around them and Rod Campbell has been particularly successful in incorporating different textures into his various books for infants. In this one, Fluffy Chick's soft, warm

Upto 18 months

feathers can be stroked on the cover while inside there is also the chance to run fingers over a lamb's woolly coat, a pig's hairy ear and a cow's rough, red tongue. But the last picture shows nothing to stroke at all, until readers finally get round to lifting up mother hen's wing. There they will discover Fluffy Chick taking a well-earned rest but still available for stroking. All the pictures in this book are bright and lively, with animal characters who – unlike the real thing – are happy to stand absolutely still while allowing young readers to take the sort of liberties with them that would often be resented in real life.

Fuzzy Yellow Ducklings
Matthew Van Fleet (illustrator)
Ragged Bears (board)

This book offers a skilful combination of textures, colours, shapes and animals in a format full of surprises. A fuzzy circle with a raised, fluffy surface on the opening page turns into a duckling when a flap is lifted and then spread out. On the next page, a bumpy brown triangle becomes part of a family of toads, perched on or around a crop of toadstools. And so it goes on, with squares, ovals and other easy shapes, each one with different textures to touch, finally revealing themselves as part of an animal. The last page contains a pull-out section where all the different animals, shapes and colours come together in a good-humoured parade. Though babies may not be that interested in rectangles or crescents at this age, they will certainly enjoy the different textures on display and the intriguing way in which smaller shapes are integrated into much larger ones. Published in a tough, board edition and using strong, stiff paper, this book is built to last and gives excellent value.

Home: Touch and Feel
Dorling Kindersley (board)

This little board book concentrates on textures found at home, from Teddy's fluffy tummy to a soft cotton curtain and a rough towel. Lift these last two, and there are flowers and butterflies behind. On the last page the question is "And who's that in the smooth, shiny mirror?" Looking to the opposite page, children will see their own faces reflected in the glass substitute. Pictures are generally more realistic in this book than is usual for this age group, but without being over-complex or

Upto 18 months

having too much detail. There are many other books in this series, including one on clothes where babies can touch anything from a pair of rough dungarees to a jaunty pink feather stuck in a pirate's hat.

Other Touch and Feel Books	
Baby Animals	Animal Colours
Kitten	Shapes
123	Clothes
ABC	Puppy

Jungle Sounds
Colin and Jacqui Hawkins
Walker Books (pb)

"Snarl! Snort! Snap! Hiss! Can *you* make jungle sounds like this?" The answer to this question will probably depend on how successfully the adult reader has managed to reproduce these same sounds in the text itself. There is no story as such but instead a series of picture showing little creatures teasing bigger ones before being chased away with a loud warning. When this finally comes it is reproduced in huge, black letters, as if demanding an appropriately loud rendition from the reader. But so long as infants know when such noises are about to happen, they can enjoy hearing them to the full without any sense of shock. And although the big animals in this book do sometimes seem to lose their tempers, they still look more amused than angry and as such are unlikely to frighten anyone small. The authors have written many books for small children, illustrated in the same jokey way that makes this book such a pleasure.

Let's Make a Noise
Amy MacDonald (author) **Maureen Roffey** (illustrator)
Walker Books (board)

Noises of all sorts are always very popular with babies, who can sometimes make passable imitations of familiar sounds even before they are able to speak. In this board

Upto 18 months

book a dog, train, cat, truck and sheep all feature in Maureen Roffey's delightfully clear and forthright illustrations. The text suggests what noises they each make, allowing adult readers to decide what exactly "BRMM, BRMM" for the truck or "TOOT, TOOT" for the train might actually sound like. The last picture shows a bawling baby, with "WAAAAH" suggested for the accompanying sound, thus allowing babies a chance to imitate themselves. Should they fail to do so, parents are likely to have no problem in reproducing this particularly noise from their own recent experience.

Lorraine Kelly Fun-to-Learn: Colours
Lynne Breeze (illustrator)
André Deutsch (board)

Babies learn from play, and this little board book is eye-catching enough to ensure the sort of attention that can lead to learning. Each page is drenched in a single colour which is also represented by an object, such as a strawberry for "red" or a banana for "yellow". Adults going through this book with a

baby will probably find themselves adding an extra layer of the sort of make-believe that makes books more memorable at this age. Obvious ideas could include investing the green telephone with a ringing noise, pretending to smell the orange flower, going through the motions of drinking from the pink cup or miming stroking the brown cat. There are no rules and you should feel free to react to the pictures in your own way when there is no text to suggest exactly how each page should be read. The reference to learning in the title does not mean that other books at this age inevitably have less to do with acquiring knowledge. Every book a baby comes across has something to offer them, particularly when your own special effects and suggestions are added. In this way, the book can also turn into something of a dialogue, with parent and baby playing a role in exchanges that could turn into well-loved rituals. Other *Lorraine Kelly Fun-to-Learn* books include *Numbers, Shapes* and *Opposites*.

My First Book of Opposites
Kim Deegan (illustrator)
Bloomsbury (hb)

Each page in this picture book is given over to one word with its opposite appearing on the other side. Within each picture the same beaming toddler

Upto 18 months

illustrates opposites such as "short" and "tall", with the help of suitably expressive illustrations. Many of the opposites cry out for special effects to be added by the reader. "Up/down", for example, lends itself perfectly to sudden movements in either direction of the type babies have always loved. "Quiet/loud" are surely meant to come over in the manner of the words themselves, while "asleep/awake", with which the book ends, could lead to some heart-felt miming. Babies need all the extra clues they can get when first coming across books, and you should never feel constrained when it comes to adding the kind of extra expression which will almost certainly result in greater enjoyment.

Peekaboo Friends!
by Lucy Su (author/illustrator)
Frances Lincoln (hb)

Robbie is looking for his toys, all of which are hidden but with enough of them still showing to indicate where they are. A pair of ears sticking out of the top of a Wellington boot reveals – on the opening of a flap – a toy giraffe. More flaps and imperfectly hidden toys follow until Robbie decides to hide them all plus himself under his bedspread. This is an artful little book, giving small readers enough clues as to where all the toys are hiding so that they will easily be able to work the puzzle out for themselves. The inclusion of flaps can be problematic in books for the very young, with even the strongest designs not always solid enough to survive enthusiastic handling. Here it wouldn't be a disaster if some flaps end up torn off, since Lucy Su's pictures are brilliant enough to stand on their own. The text is an accumulative one, with each page introducing another character to those already looking for their hidden friends. From traditional rhymes like "Who Killed Cock Robin?" onwards, accumulative stories have always offered small children an entertaining way of testing and

Upto 18 months

developing their powers of memory, and accompanying pictures make the task of remembering a growing list of characters that much easier and enjoyable.

Peek-a-Boo!
Jan Ormerod (illustrator)
Bodley Head (board)

Peek-a-boo must be the most popular baby game ever. This popularity has much to do with how babies' perceptual skills develop, and the way they initially believe that if something cannot be seen then it can't be there. Games of peek-a-boo which show them familiar objects appearing and disappearing in quick succession offer them a way of experimenting with this idea and eventually challenging it for themselves, although why infants find such games so funny at the same time has never been satisfactorily explained. Whatever the truth, books that play similar games can also be very popular, with this one a good case in point. Affectionately illustrated by Jan Ormerod, each page shows a baby playing peek-a-boo by holding up something in front of his or her face. When a flap is lowered readers can now see the same baby in full. So for those moments when parents feel too tired to play this ancient game with their babies themselves, there is now a book that does the task for them.

Tickle, Tickle
Helen Oxenbury (illustrator)
Walker Books (board)

Helen Oxenbury is a brilliant illustrator, and in this picture book she captures to perfection the look of comfortable, contented roundness babies have on those days when they seem more than usually happy with life. Babies are pictured crawling through mud, playing in the sea, having their hair brushed (not usually a moment for good humour) and finally being tickled by two older children and a mother. The short accompanying text is in rhyme, and although there are only five thick board pages these are still more than enough to establish a warm, loving atmosphere. Parents could also look out for the same illustrator's *Say Goodnight, Clap Hands* and *All Fall Down,* published in the same series and equally enchanting.

Where Does Maisy Live?
Lucy Cousins (illustrator)
Walker Books (board)

Upto 18 months

This simple board book features Maisy, a jovial mouse character. She disappears after the first page, leaving readers with the task of lifting up various flaps on different dwelling places – hen house, pigsty, kennel and stable – to see if this is where Maisy is now living. In every case the answer is "No", since all these

places are already occupied. But on the last page there is a house with a large green door which, when opened, reveals Maisy in her usual outfit of blue dungarees, striped shirt and red boots. Many other books also exist about her, all with the same bright colours and child-friendly forms, and with each shape surrounded by a thick black line in the way made famous by the Dutch artist Dick Bruna. Lucy Cousins is his worthy successor – inventive, witty and always right on a child's wavelength.

Upto 18 months

Ten More Maisy Books

Maisy's Favourite
Animals
Maisy at the Farm
Maisy Likes Driving
Maisy Goes to
Playschool
Maisy Dresses Up

Maisy Goes to Bed
Maisy Makes
Gingerbread
Maisy Goes Swimming
Maisy's Bedtime
Maisy's Favourite
Clothes

Whose Baby Am I?

John Butler (author/illustrator)

Viking Books (hb) Puffin Books (pb)

Wildlife illustrator John Butler, here brings his talents
to a picture book depicting animals exactly as they
would be after a good bath and plenty of grooming.
The overall idea is ingenious, starting on the first page
with a fluffy looking chick with enormous eyes asking
the question, "Whose baby am I?" Turn the page, and
readers see the little owlet safely with his mother. On
the opposite page is another lost baby, this time a small
elephant who is reunited with his mother over the page.
So it goes on with a koala bear, a giraffe, a seal, a panda
and various other baby animals. Printed on sturdy card
pages rather than
boards, this
excellent picture
book finishes on
a two-page
spread, one
showing all
the babies
involved and the
other all the
mothers. The
question is then
put, "Can you

Upto 18 months

guess whose baby is whose?" Small children should not find this too difficult, and may well enjoy the extra time spent on this captivating book. Its theme of a baby's need for its mother is also highly relevant to children at the same stage of life themselves.

The Wibbly Pig Collection
Mick Inkpen (illustrator)
Hodder (board)

Wibbly Pig is a stout, pink, young pig who enjoys life to the full. This attractive series of board books doesn't so much tell stories about him as present him in a series of situations recognizable to small children. In one he is seen enjoying all his favourite things – from eating bananas to going on the swing – in another he paints pictures, while in a third he dances, bounces and sings. The text sometimes asks whether readers enjoy doing the same sort of thing, and even babies without much language will probably want to nod their agreement. With five of these titles (*Wibbly Pig is Happy*, *…Can Dance*, *…Likes Bananas*, *…Opens his Presents*, *…Can Make a Tent*) sharing the same neat little box, children are introduced to the whole idea of a series of books, each one resembling the other but different in terms of what they are actually about. Sturdily bound and small enough to fit easily into a small child's hands, these books readily deserve their huge popularity with little children.

First Stories

For very young children enjoying a story involves a number of complex intellectual skills. In order to make sense of its middle and end, for example, they must be able to remember its beginning, just as they have to keep track of characters who appear more than once. It is also important that they understand the words used and can make sense of the accompanying pictures and how they relate to the story. Lastly, they must be able to see why a story ends when it does, and what exactly it was all about. Without such understanding, stories can be little more than strings of unrelated words and pictures passing over a child's head while he or she is thinking about something else.

Most humans are born with a propensity for understanding and enjoying stories, and fiction in some form or other crops up in every known culture. There are good reasons for this, since stories have always acted as one important way in which anyone – young or old –

Upto 18 months

can learn through the imagination what they cannot always discover from real life. But first the child needs to relate one incident to another so that the whole thing hangs together in their own mind as well as on the printed page. No wonder, then, that children often ask so many questions while they are hearing a story and sometimes want to hear the same old tales over and over again until they can finally be sure what exactly they are all about.

Bathwater's Hot

Shirley Hughes (author/illustrator)
Walker Books (hb & pb)

Shirley Hughes found working on this picture book "concentrated and exhausting because it was like actually being with a very small child". Certainly there is no better illustrator than her at catching the sense of noise, mess and movement of children having a good time with each other. The two main characters here are a baby brother and a slightly older sister. Sets of rhyming opposites illustrate such eternal truths as

Upto 18 months

"Night time is dark / Day time is light. The sun says 'good morning'/ And the moon says 'goodnight.'" But it is the pictures that really matter, from cluttered bathrooms wreathed in steam to a children's party with a certain amount of grabbing and pushing going on in the background. The children in this book are no angels, and even the beaming baby is seen getting into mischief. But a sense of pleasure and excitement simply at being alive is always there too, caught by an artist whose pictures of modern family life are instantly recognizable as well as consistently delightful.

Cat is Sleepy
Satoshi Kitamura (illustrator)
Andersen Press (board)

Cats tend to get a good press in children's books, with an emphasis upon their cuddly side rather than on their less pleasing characteristics. But the cat in this board picture book although benign is definitely no charmer. His lugubrious face instead exudes the world-weariness of a pet who can find nowhere quiet enough to enjoy the sleep he has been looking forward to. Each room that he visits has too many disadvantages – from a bedroom cluttered with toys to a drawing room resonating with the sounds of inexpert piano practice. Finally Cat finds a cosy place on a little girl's lap, and settles down to sleep with the nearest he ever gets to a smile on his face. Satoshi Kitamura is a leading illustrator, and this book shows why. No one else has ever drawn a cat quite like this one, and yet the permanently despairing animal gazing out from these pages is immediately recognizable as well as very funny.

Going Shopping
Sarah Garland (illustrator)
Bodley Head (board)

Mum, daughter, baby and dog are all beaming on the cover of this board book, but once inside the whole exhausting business of going out for a big shop in the car is depicted in all its grim reality. The baby looks happy enough, finally going to sleep in the supermarket trolley before being carried to the car by a distinctly flustered Mum

along with all the heavy shopping. The daughter looks
pretty tired by this point, and it is precisely this note of
determined reality that makes the book so successful.
Although Mum's Morris Minor Estate looks dated,
everything else rings as true now as when the book was
first published in 1982. Small children will enjoy all its
abundant detail, while parents and older children with
more experience of such shopping trips will smile in
sheer recognition of the hurly-burly so expertly caught
by Sarah Garland. This author-artist has designed other
books about the same family where things are a little
less fraught, particularly in *Having a Picnic* and *Going
Swimming*. Either of them would make an interesting
contrast to this enjoyable little book.

Puppy
Rachel O'Neill (illustrator)
Michael O'Mara Books (board)

This is one of those board books made in the shape of
the animal it is about. So as well as reading about Patch
the Puppy, readers can pick him up once the book is
closed and its puppy shape becomes more obvious.
Inside the pages Patch looks for someone to play with
and after various refusals ends up with Billy, a small
boy also looking for a game. Rachel O'Neill's
illustrations are bright and jolly, and further

Upto 18 months

publications in this Animal Shape series include Guinea Pig, Rabbit and Kitten. These titles, along with others that also diverge from the normal book shape, all serve to stretch childrens' concept of what a book actually is and help them associate the act of reading with fun.

Sleepyhead

Nicola Smee (author/illustrator)

Campbell Books (board)

"Time for bed, / sleepyhead. / Bathtime's over, / story's read." With this story, babies should sleep extra well, lulled by the comforting and affectionate atmosphere evident on every one of its seven thick pages. Each shows a baby getting a stage further to bed, until the longed-for moment finally arrives. Tucked into a crib, there is one surprise still to come, in the shape of a raised green blanket which gives

Upto 18 months

young readers the chance to touch and feel its particular texture. A kitten, a toy mouse and a teddy bear also appear, but it is the baby who is centre-stage, very sleepy by the end but before that still up for play when being helped into a pair of yellow pyjamas. Nicola Smee uses soft colours for a story that is gentleness personified.

Upto 18 months

Younger toddlers

18 months to 2¹/₂

Younger toddlers

18 months to 2$^{1}/_{2}$

Although children at eighteen months are never fluent speakers, they can still get a great deal out of simple stories and pictures. Beginning by identifying particular objects in illustrations and anticipating some of the words in favourite texts, they gradually move on to enjoying whole – if very short – stories. Books for this age tend to stick to the familiar, leaving more obvious fantasy for slightly older readers, and illustrators usually cut down on extraneous detail in order to help inexperienced eyes focus on main objects and events. Colours are often bright, and objects drawn in clear, bold lines.

Although children will now be learning new words all the time, they will always understand more than they will be able to utter, which is why stories and poems start getting really popular at this age. A story offers an infant a set order of words which never varies (unlike human speech) and pictures that are essentially static (unlike TV images). Hearing a popular story repeated several times offers small children a chance to familiarize themselves with complex material that is also entertaining and attractive.

Favourite stories for this age-group may look fairly simple but the demands they make upon infants are still considerable. This explains why they usually have a limited cast of characters, with the action made as obvious as possible. Sub-plots (where another story exists alongside the main one) will have to wait until a later age, along with characters who change and develop. Books that ask difficult questions of readers, are also inappropriate at an age when readers still have many difficult questions of their own to ask of stories – not least what they are all actually about.

Other popular books at this age may not involve stories at all. Nursery rhymes and poems offer the traditional appeal of strong rhyme and rhythm, while counting or alphabet books concentrate on objects rather than events. What all books for this age do tend to have in common is the presence of bright pictures and a cheerful text with the hope of making a child's first contact with books as much fun as possible. High quality, entertaining pop-up or flap-lifting books help in particular to spread this message, along with a variety of other early books that use ingenious special effects.

Favourite characters for this age are often humanized animals who go through a range of adventures before everything ends happily. Very often these adventures involve ordinary parent-child interactions, but made universal by the fact that animal characters stand outside all human hierarchies, countries and classifications and can therefore be easily identified with by all types of reader.

18 months to 2¹/₂

Nursery Rhymes

Most nursery rhymes were never composed with children especially in mind. More often, a mother, nursemaid or whoever would simply find themselves singing the first thing that came to mind when soothing children or playing with them. Thus fragments from bawdy songs or country ballads would be passed from one generation to the next as children became parents themselves, their repetitions, rhymes and strong rhythms having made them particularly easy to remember. In some cases such rhymes are linked with particular games, like riding on an adult's knee and then pretending to fall. Others focus on parts of a child's body, such as toes, nose and fingers, often accompanied by tickling games. During all this time, infants will be picking up vocabulary and grammatical structures, as well as a few chunks of more formal learning like the days of the week, the months of the year, counting, the alphabet or the difference between left and right.

So far as the imagination is concerned, nursery rhymes have a limitless appeal for young children. They contain both sense and nonsense, plus a huge range of topics including really important ones like birth, love and death. They can also feature violence, and most infants will welcome rhymes that recognize some of their own occasional capacity for aggression. Many are about the utterly mundane, such as going to bed, losing and finding things, eating meals and playing. Others deal with the most exaggerated nonsense imaginable, with giant-sized eggs falling off walls, dishes running away with spoons – ideas which are memorable partly because they are so unexpected. Like the rest of us, small children enjoy both the literature of the everyday and of the fantastic. In nursery rhymes they get both.

Most important of all is the actual language nursery rhymes employ. For the poet Walter de la Mare, they offered "a short cut into poetry itself". The fact that some phrases are nonsense ("Higgledy-piggledy"), some phrases are archaic ("cock-horse") and some whole rhymes are completely inexplicable ("Pop goes the weasel") is, paradoxically, one of nursery rhymes' greatest strengths. For as well as turning to words for meaning, infants are also interested in words simply for the sound they make – and nursery rhymes contain some of the finest-sounding words it is possible to imagine.

Those chosen below represent a few out of very many, where it seems to me the artist has complemented the rhymes in a particularly effective way.

The Dorling Kindersley Book of Nursery Rhymes

Debi Gliori (illustrator)
Dorling Kindersley (hb)

This collection concentrates on old favourites, but sometimes slips in a short explanation as to what exactly some rhymes are really about. So "cock-horse" is defined here as a toy horse, with a picture to match, and "pease pudding" is explained as thin soup made from mashed peas. Elsewhere children may be relieved to know that the pig eaten by Tom the Piper's son was not in fact a real animal but a pastry pig filled with currants. However, the artist is wrong when she repeats the common belief that "Ring-a-ring o' roses" has something to do with the Great Plague. As Peter and Iona Opie have pointed out in their famous dictionary, this particular rhyme was going the rounds long before the plague came to Britain. Its origins have more to do with children's age-old enjoyment in simply linking hands, going round in circles and then falling down together with a bump.

But this is the only thing this gifted illustrator does get wrong in this otherwise perfect book. Set very much in the contemporary world, hot cross buns are baked in a modern-looking kitchen while Polly puts the kettle on after playing in her sandpit. Boy and girl characters are pictured very much as they look now, cropping up in a variety of strange situations but still equal to anything that Mother Goose can throw at them. In the countryside scenes, the houses look modern, lit by electricity instead of by candles. Every now and again photographs of real children creep in, somehow finding a space between the decorated borders and the plethora of detail that already adorn this book. Debi Gliori writes in her introduction that putting it all together was rather like sewing a patchwork quilt. This is a good analogy, for this book too is warm, cosy, colourful and just the thing for a small child either going to bed or else waking up next morning.

18 months to 2½

Each Peach Pear Plum

Allan Ahlberg (author)
Janet Ahlberg (illustrator)
Viking (hb)
Puffin Books (pb)

This lovely little book is not a nursery rhyme collection as such, but it does feature a whole cast of characters well known to Mother Goose. It is included here for children who have got to know some of these people for themselves, and might enjoy working out where exactly they are hiding on the page. The first picture invites readers to join in a game of "I Spy" – in this case, for Tom Thumb, pictured sitting in a tree. Over the page he's now perched in a cupboard, but where is Mother Hubbard? Many more games of "I Spy" follow – for Bo Peep, almost hidden in a field, Jack and Jill, whose legs can be seen in mid-fall, and Baby Bunting, who makes two appearances in his cradle. Elsewhere characters wander in and out of each other's pages at will, ending up all crammed together on a picnic eating a giant plum pie. The illustrations by Janet Ahlberg are, as always, highly detailed, witty and filled with visual jokes and cross-references – some of which only become clear after repeated readings.

Lucy Cousins' Book of Nursery Rhymes
Lucy Cousins (illustrator)
Macmillan (hb)

There are only eighteen rhymes in this book, but there's enough energy in Lucy Cousins' pictures to illustrate another hundred or so. She draws and paints rather like children themselves, producing pictures of stiff-armed, manically smiling characters splattered across the page in a way that parents and grandparents used to more conventional art-work may not always like. Children, on the

other hand, feel immediately at home with these illustrations, in which everything is giant-sized – including some of the lettering on the page. The broad, black outlines make these pictures easy for young eyes to pick out, especially when they are set against backgrounds of colour wash or sometimes just plain,

18 months to 2½

blank paper. It is difficult to get through this book without smiling, and there can be no better way of experiencing nursery rhymes.

Michael Foreman's Nursery Rhymes
Michael Foreman (illustrator)
Walker Books (hb)

This anthology, with a foreword by Iona Opie, is illustrated by one of Britain's foremost children's illustrators. Michael Foreman begins this book with babies waking up ("Hush-a-bye, baby") and finishes it 150 pages later with older children going to bed ("How many miles to Babylon?") In between there are lullabies, action rhymes, nonsense verse, riddles and tongue-twisters, all tumbling over each other for the reader's attention. Links are made between particular rhymes, with the "Grand Old Duke of York" marching up to the top of the hill and "Jack and Jill" falling down its other side at the turn of a page. Both pictures are typical of Foreman's technical mastery. The red-coated soldiers with their bright flags and yellow rifles, make a colourful spectacle as they march by, although they mean little to the old woman who lived under a hill who is pictured quietly drinking a cup of tea on the same page. Jack and Jill, by contrast, are dressed in rather boring clothes, with all the attention going to movement and Jack's subsequent patching up before the two children end up playing seesaw across a gate.

Once again, animal characters share the honours with human ones against a background where sea, fields and cottages mingle into a vision of rural perfection. One or two slightly scary moments (a mean-looking giant, a cat slavering with clearly evil intent in front of a mouse's hole) make sure there is always a balance between the sweet and the occasionally slightly sour. Cock Robin still dies but many other characters have a really good time, culminating in a magnificent four-page spread illustrating the twelve days of Christmas. With over 200 rhymes to choose from, and many more bright, ingenious pictures accompanying them, this is another book to treasure.

My Very First Mother Goose
Iona Opie (editor) **Rosemary Wells** (illustrator)
Walker Books (hb & pb)

Iona Opie is the undisputed world authority on Mother Goose and co-author with her late husband Peter of the famous *Oxford Dictionary of Nursery Rhymes*. In a short preface to this enchanting anthology, she says more about these rhymes than many others have managed in ten times the space. For her, nursery rhymes teach readers not to be "put out by life's little bumps and

18 months to 2½

bruises". Instead, they suggest "that mishaps might be funny rather than tragic, that tantrums can be comical as well as frightening, and that laughter is the cure for practically everything". When small children fall over, as they always will, this is only to be expected given the knowledge that Jack and Jill fell down too. A grizzling child can be taken out of themselves by a happy dance; another child not wanting to go to bed might feel better once they have the idea that they are really

marching "Up the wooden hill to Blanket Fair".

The American illustrator Rosemary Wells provides a series of glowing watercolours. Most of her characters are household animals, always useful to an illustrator as a way of avoiding indications of nationality, ethnic group or social class. With rhymes as universal as these, it is fitting to illustrate them with symbols that are universal too. Any fixed sense of period in her pictures is also vague, with cars and aeroplanes sharing space with men going to plough and horse-drawn carts. Most rhymes are familiar, but some are not, reminding readers that there is no such thing as a fixed repertoire of these verses. As Iona Opie has written elsewhere, if parents know any rhyme in a slightly different form, or indeed have their own favourites unknown to anyone else, these are just as valid as any choice made by an anthologist.

This is a collection full of colour and bursting with energy, that takes infants into worlds sometimes familiar, sometimes bizarre but always interesting. It is a very handsome but not a particularly cheap volume, and parents might squirm if they see it being roughly treated. But love of books at a young age always has a potentially destructive side to it, and if this volume gets to look battered over the years this may be testament to how much it has been both used and loved.

Skip Across the Ocean:
Nursery Rhymes from Around the World

Floella Benjamin (editor) **Sheila Moxley** (illustrator)

Frances Lincoln (hb)

Every country has its own store of nursery rhymes. This is not surprising, given that babies love the sound of the human voice and have always been pacified by it. Floella Benjamin, originally from the Caribbean, has attempted to bring together nursery rhyme examples

18 months to 2½

from around the world in one collection. The best of her selection has a common background in English, whether drawn from America, Ireland, Australia or Trinidad. Rhymes from other countries appear in translations, sometimes losing some of their magic on the way. But by including overseas nursery rhyme versions in their original languages this book does have a genuine, international feel to it. For small infants, it will be enough simply to hear these rhymes. When they are older, they may want to ask questions about some of the different

things going on in the text. What exactly is a kookaburra, a cowrie shell or a carp streamer, for instance? Fortunately, Sheila Moxley's luminous illustrations are packed with enough detail to help out all parents who may not know the answers to such questions themselves.

This Little Puffin
Elizabeth Matterson (editor) **Claudio Muñoz** (illustrator)
Puffin Books (pb)

This collection of nursery rhymes, songs and games is a treasury that every household containing small children should acquire. Published over twenty years ago, it has long since proved its worth in Mother-and-Baby Groups, Day Centres, Play Groups, Nursery Schools and homes across the country. Revised and updated, it continues to provide songs and rhymes for every occasion. Relevant tunes are sometimes added in single stave form, easy enough for any adult with a basic knowledge of musical notation to pick out on a piano or play on a recorder.

As Elizabeth Matterson points out, there is a limit to the amount of meaningful direct conversation possible with very small children during an ordinary day. Songs and rhymes, therefore, provide perfect, non-demanding ways of communicating with youngsters while also creating a happy and relaxed atmosphere. Or as she

18 months to 2¹/2

puts it herself, "Most households develop their own repertoire of bedtime and silly-time songs. There are other times when singing can distract a frightened child, change the mood of a fretful child and can while away tedious experiences such as journeys or waiting times when no other activity is possible."

Starting with Baby Games (Tickly rhymes, Peep-Bo and so on) this book then works its way through Special Occasions (Christmas and birthdays) to Follow my Leader, Farm Songs and Some Special People ("Yankee Doodle", "John Brown" and many others). For parents anxious about how best to pass the next few hours at their next toddler's birthday party, this book is particularly recommended. Merely working through its final section on Singing and Dancing will use up most of the time in as nice a way as possible – and all at no extra expense.

18 months to 2½

Counting Books

Children often learn to count out loud from one to ten quite quickly, sometimes helped by various traditional rhymes and games. But learning how to count objects in front of them takes longer, given that the whole concept of number is a difficult one to grasp. One common confusion is to do with appearance: small children can often believe that a few beads spread out in front of them amount to more than a greater number of beads grouped together in a smaller space. An ability to think clearly about problems such as this may not be fully established until the age of five or after. It is a process that cannot really be hurried, and children need to take their own time over it.

It is also true that when older infants feel really involved in a counting situation – for example over who might be getting the most sweets – they often manage to come to more accurate conclusions. Counting Books that offer them a range of interesting opportunities to play with different numbers in an attractive and diverting way can play an important role in encouraging number skills. It is also important for future learning that infants' first encounters with numbers should be pleasurable rather than threatening: unsympathetic Counting Books that demand too much too early could turn into a hindrance rather than a help. The following books are recommended, more for their fun content than as teaching aids. The best Counting Books offer children a chance to learn about numbers at their own speed and in their own way, so that when they get to school, numbers will seem like friends rather than enemies.

Alfie's Numbers
Shirley Hughes (illustrator)
Red Fox (pb) Bodley Head (board)

Alfie and Annie Rose are two of Shirley Hughes's best-loved child characters, and in this picture book they wander together through the first ten numbers. They start off with two on a seesaw, and then move up to three over the page when Alfie's friends come round to play, leaving Annie Rose feeling rather left out. Some numbers are illustrated more than once, with "3" also pictured describing Alfie, his dad and a pig. The scene here is a family camping trip, with the pig in question nosing around a tent which Dad and Alfie are trying to sleep in at night. The same sense of domestic intimacy in sometimes unpredictable circumstances runs throughout this book, which also includes five people going to a party, six sitting round the table and seven friendly neighbours enjoying a cup of tea. The impression is one of peeping in at real people all doing the sort of ordinary – and occasionally extraordinary – things that happen in the course of family life. The only break with everyday reality comes when Alfie's cereal bowl is shown with nine messy bears walking round its rim rather than lying as flat decorations. This is in no sense an organized counting-book. Instead it travels gently from 1 to 10 taking in a few pleasant diversions on the way and sometimes stopping altogether for a little chat with its readers, whether young or old. As an introduction to numbers, its sheer good humour and meandering charm could end up making it far more memorable and user-friendly than many more logical Counting Books.

18 months to 2½

57

Engines, Engines: an Indian Counting Rhyme

Lisa Bruce (illustrator)

Bloomsbury (pb)

18 months to 2½

Ten different engines feature in this picture book, illustrated by Stephen Waterhouse in full technicolour and then some. Engine Number One sets off in the midday sun and engine Number Two goes past the temple of Vishnu until finally engine Number Ten follows the Ganges home again. In between there are dancing women wearing bright saris, camels, elephants, naughty monkeys and a fabulous palace with a golden gate. Colours glisten like jewels, gleaming in a sun that only disappears during a magical, moonlit journey across the Himalayas. Children often enjoy train stories from an early age, and this one takes the genre into almost impossibly romantic surroundings. Counting itself is represented not just by the rhymes but also by the number of carriages each engine pulls. On the last page the rhyme reads: "The journey's finished, our fun is done / To travel again, go back to ONE!" Many young readers will surely do just that, in order to experience once again the sensual wonders displayed so generously on every page.

Fruits: A Caribbean Counting Poem

Valerie Bloom (author) **David Axtell** (illustrator)

Caribbean Publishing (hb) Macmillan (pb)

Here is a counting book with a difference. It's set in the Caribbean and uses words such as "guinep" (a small fruit) and "smaddy" (somebody), all explained in a short, accompanying glossary. Its pictures and rhymes will be as enticing to non-Caribbean readers as the ten different fruits that crop up in a story revolving around a resourceful bigger girl and a little sister determined not to be left out. Each page shows another step in the plot to get hold of some of the fruit against the wishes of parents, who are only ever seen in the

background. Will it be a question of picking one guinep from the tree and coming back at night to take the "two ripe guava pon the shelf", or stealing just one big bite from the three "sweet-sop" in a fruit basket left by a temptingly open window? All these ingenious plans finally collapse when, after eating ten bananas, the older girl – now looking distinctly queasy – begs her sister to "Mek me lie down on me bed, quick, / Lawd, ah

18 months to 2½

feeling really sick." Her little sister, who has eaten much less, looks on with sympathy mixed with curiosity. With wonderful illustrations by David Axtell, full of sun and sly, good humour, this book is a reminder that one way of learning how to count has always involved either something being eaten or – in the case of fruit stones – something left at the side of the plate.

How Many Bugs in a Box?
A Lift-up Counting Book

David A. Carter (illustrator)

Orchard Books (hb)

This book gets wilder and wilder as it progresses from one tough bug hidden away in a red box to ten crazed insects all trying to saw their way out of a pop-up packing case with "Open if you dare" printed on the front. Opening and shutting the page simply makes them saw away all the faster. Before that there are three pretty butterflies, five frightened fish bugs, whose fins move when their particular flap is

opened, and six hungry frog-bugs all of whose tongues are attached to a luckless fly. Since the book contains various small parts, there is a warning that it is not suitable for children under three years of age. But it would probably not last long anyhow if it were ever exposed to the natural destructiveness of any small child intent on finding out how pop-up books actually work. With suitable adult supervision though, this is certainly a book to cherish, whether it also manages to teach young readers anything about counting or not.

Nine More Bug Books

More Bugs in Boxes	The Twelve Bugs of
Feely Bugs	Christmas
Alpha Bugs	Giggle Bugs
Easter Bugs	Bedtime Bugs
Space Bugs	Glitter Bugs

How Many Monsters?
A Monster Counting Book

Mara van der Meer (author/illustrator)

Frances Lincoln (hb & pb)

These monsters are so much like little boys and girls having a bad day, that even the most timid child will find nothing to be frightened of. The reader is invited

18 months to 2½

to answer a series of increasingly personal questions such as "How many smelly feet has this monster got?" or "How many monsters are picking their noses?" Elsewhere another monster tries to scare six grannies but ends up frightened himself, hiding under the bed with nine other friends. Each page has a flap which, when lifted, answers various "How many?" questions from number of flowers

picked (7) to cakes stolen (9). By the time all ten monsters line up to wave goodbye to their readers at the end of this book they have all become increasingly amiable friends. The artist-author possesses a good line in visual humour, and is never afraid to use big, splashy colours to create various comic monster effects. Most children will enjoy the sometimes rather gross humour found in this story, and may well learn something useful about counting at the same time.

Little Miss Muffet Counts to Ten

Emma Chichester Clark (author/illustrator)

Andersen Press (hb) Red Fox (pb)

Children who already know about Little Miss Muffet
will notice straightaway that something different is
going on here. The big spider now asks her to stay, and
then, over the page, "Along came two lemurs, / With
trumpets and streamers, / And bunting to make a
display." These in turn are followed by three magpies,
four foxes and five pussycats, ending up more
ominously with ten crocodiles bearing a large box and
greedy smiles. But there is nothing to worry about,
since the box contains a birthday cake for everyone to
celebrate Miss Muffet's birthday, which happens to be
on that day. Emma Chichester Clark illustrates her own
rhymes with all the inventiveness and humour she
brings to her other picture books. As the pages become
more cluttered, with each new band of arrivals joining
the last batch, things become increasingly manic and
more surreal as the various animals rush about. Even
the crocodiles turn out to be everyone's friends, joining
in the final wild dance. Certainly Miss Muffet herself
will never seem quite the same again, and if some of
this cheerfulness also rubs off on to the accompanying
numbers writ large on each page, so much the better.

18 months to 2½

My First Book of Numbers
Kim Deegan (illustrator)
Bloomsbury (hb)

Using extra-strong paper designed to withstand small
hands, this colourful picture book counts down from
ten to one, with every number printed in such huge
type that a toddler could stand on each of them with
room to spare. Skittles, bricks, crayons and other child-
friendly objects all feature without ever being named,
and a written text only appears on the last two pages.
There we see an indignant-looking mum, hands on
hips, looking on at "One big mess!" This is composed
of every object pictured before spread out over the
floor, with the boy seen on the previous pages there as
well, smiling proudly at the scene of epic untidiness he's
managed to create. Leaving children to make their own
sense of each page, this is a Counting Book with
minimal teaching overtones and maximum charm – an
excellent combination for readers still at an early stage
of number awareness.

One, Two, Guess Who?
Colin and Jacqui Hawkins
Harper Collins (hb & pb)

"One, Two, what a to-do! / 'We'll lock you out,' the

18 months to 2¹/₂

Little Pigs shout. / Who blew down the house of twigs, / And frightened away the Three Little Pigs?" For the answer to this question, it is necessary to unfold a flap at the end of each facing page. Asked then to choose between Puss in Boots, the Big Bad Wolf and the Beast, as the more likely villain, well-read infants will surely opt for the wolf – revealed, surely enough, inside the flap, puffing away at the famous house of bricks. And so this pleasant little book goes on, finishing at number ten and drawing on other well-known fairy tale characters along the way. Counting skills are supported by linked rows of objects – three hats and four cats for Cinderella, for example – which appear at the bottom of each page and are grouped together at the end. Accompanying illustrations are always good fun, cluttered with detail inside each house but expansive and lyrical whenever the action takes place outside.

18 months to 2½

Spot Can Count
Eric Hill (author/illustrator)
Frederick Warne (hb) Puffin Books (pb)

Spot the Puppy decides to count all the animals on the

farm with the help of his dad. On the second page, behind a sack that is also a lift-up flap, he finds a mouse. On the next page he lifts a clump of leaves from a tree and there, answering the question "How many squirrels?" is a large figure 2 for all to see. And so it goes on, with the exact number of whatever animals are being counted always hidden behind a flap that only reveals its secret when it's raised. Infants going through this little book can either count the animals on each page for themselves or else lift the flap and read out the number. Accompanying illustrations are bright and cheerful, with occasional speech bubbles carrying on the story in a pleasantly inconsequential way. If the flaps eventually get torn off, the numbers themselves (written in letters as well as appearing as numerals) will still show through. Spot the Puppy has proved popular with readers in many other books written and illustrated by Eric Hill, and enlisting this lively character on the side of numeracy in such a skilful and unobtrusive manner is an excellent idea.

Ten, Nine, Eight

Molly Bang (author/illustrator)
Red Fox (pb)

This Counting Book starts at the number ten and works down to number one when the child featured in its pages finally gets into bed. Before that moment, we see her "10 small toes all washed and warm", then over the next pages nine favourite toys, eight square

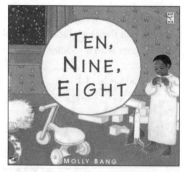

windowpanes, seven empty shoes and so on down to "1 big girl ready for bed." Dad is shown in charge of the whole operation, and a missing shoe is finally traced to the family cat, seen playing with it on another page. Though this book is recommended by the publishers for reading together at the age of two, there is also plenty here for younger children. Colours are soft, detail is nicely observed, and an atmosphere of loving affection is maintained throughout.

Wake Up/Sleep Tight
Ken Wilson-Max (author/illustrator)
Bloomsbury (board)

Learning how to tell the time is usually too advanced for this age group, but a board book such as this with a clock and moveable hands could still prove popular

18 months to 2½

while helping to teach recognition of some of the numbers on the clock face. This book, which is in two halves, starts with a toddler urging his mum and dad in

rhyme to wake up at 7 o'clock in the morning. The cardboard hands of the clock at the top are then adjusted before moving to the next page, which shows breakfast (complete with spilt milk) at eight. Other times follow – ten o'clock for shopping and four o'clock for a visit to the park. It's then necessary to reverse the book in order to reach its other section, which takes the story on to bed-time via five o'clock tea, and a seven o'clock story. By this time the children have changed from white to black, along with their parents. All the pictures are drawn with thick, bold lines within which there are generous daubs of bright colours. Even if the hands of the two clocks, front and back, do eventually fall off there is plenty else to be getting on with here, all of it pleasant to the eye as well as to the ear.

Alphabet Books

At their best, modern alphabet books can be bright, inventive and attractive. Children may indeed learn the alphabet from them, yet once again this is a process best left to the child concerned, and there should never be any sense of blame or shame if little seems to have been absorbed over time. If alphabet books are used by parents in a way that turns them into stressful chores, more may have been lost than gained. It is so much better simply to treat an alphabet book as something to be enjoyed in its own right, allowing infants all the time in the world to recognize the various letters on display. Their different shapes, so well-known to adults but to a child still strange and unfamiliar, have a much better chance of turning into old friends if they are introduced by alphabet books where each letter has the chance to become something of a character in its own right.

Children are no longer recommended to learn reading primarily through a knowledge of the alphabet. But learning to recognize certain letters early on, such as those that make up a child's initials, can help form a useful bridge between reading at home and a child's first experience of deciphering simple words at school. Learning the typical sounds that letters of the alphabet make can also be helpful. On the other hand, alphabet books can also be popular because illustrators, freed from the disciplines of needing to tell a story, can concentrate instead on achieving some of their biggest and brightest effects. A strong tradition of brilliantly illustrated alphabet books for children stretches right back to the nineteenth century and to the work of Kate Greenaway. Many modern alphabet books are equally good, in particular the titles recommended below.

Alfie's Alphabet
Shirley Hughes (illustrator)
Bodley Head (hb)

This enchanting volume is made up from pages taken from various other picture books written and illustrated by Shirley Hughes with a new, minimal text here, beginning with "A is for Alfie and his little sister, Annie Rose". Children who already know these characters will be delighted to meet them again, while those who have never come across them before will almost certainly want to find out more. As always,

18 months to 2½

Shirley Hughes illustrates ordinary children doing ordinary things like drawing, playing in the park, reading stories and splashing in puddles. Each child is caught in a pose that is immediately recognizable to anyone who has had any hands-on experience of small children themselves. F is for friends, for example, shown tumbling over each other as only small children can. Adults get a look in too, with G for grandma, taking time off from telling a story to join in a little dance with her grandchildren. There is also the mysterious world outside, as in M for moon, shown shining on Alfie's back garden, and in the process turning an everyday sight into something magical and atmospheric.

John Burningham's ABC
John Burningham (illustrator)
Jonathan Cape (board)

This book is dedicated to A.S. Neill, the great twentieth-century educator whose aim was to take all the fear out

18 months to 2¹/₂

of teaching and learning at school. He would surely have approved of this zany, rambling alphabet book, which on one typical page flits between umbrellas, an erupting volcano, a wasp and a xylophone, played by a Gallic-looking musician complete with frock coat and white tie. John Burningham combines a vivid sense of colour with a natural feeling for eccentricity, so that his birds and dogs as well as clowns and kings all come over as looking quite intriguingly odd. Printed on stiff board, this book is crammed full of things to look at (the picture of the jungle alone includes around thirty different animals). It is also a book capable of producing that quality of continuous enjoyment within which some of the best learning has always had a good chance of taking place.

Kipper's A to Z
Mick Inkpen (author/illustrator)
Hodder (hb)

Kipper the Puppy has appeared in numerous picture books by Mick Inkpen, and he is joined in these pages by his little pig friend Arnold. The two characters then wander through the alphabet in a loosely constructed story, starting with the discovery of an Ant and ending with a toy Zebra who has already made several premature attempts to get in on the act.

Each page contains one or more words starting with the same letter, some of them not particularly easy to illustrate ("on", "off", "oops") and one difficult even to pronounce ("xugglygug"). But Mick Inkpen takes a pleasantly relaxed view of his task here, using gentle humour in text and illustration while always taking a child's eye of things. When it comes to "Volcano", the two friends decide to draw one of their own in what then turns into what must be one of the messiest pages ever to appear in a picture book. Both animals play their way through this book with all the concentration and occasional bursts of merriment found in human children. Lying on their tummies and every now and again gazing into the cardboard box where they try to keep some insects, they make an endearing pair for readers of all ages.

A to Z

18 months to 2½

Some More Kipper Books

Kipper's Sticky Paws
Kipper's Sunny Day
Kipper's Book of
   Weather
Kipper and the Egg
Kipper's Book of
   Counting
Kipper's Christmas Eve
Kipper's Toybox
Kipper's Birthday

My First ABC Board Book
Dorling Kindersley (board)

Sharp-eyed infants will spot that some of the characters here are the same as those appearing in this publisher's Word Book mentioned on p.81. But the child models involved are photographed in new poses, and it is always nice for children to come across connections between one book and another – one reason, of course, why they so enjoy series books that use a stock of the same characters in illustrations and text. The technique in this alphabet book is to fill each page with animals and objects all starting with the same letter. As with the Word Book, photographs appear alongside colour illustrations, with an emphasis both on the ordinary (needle, nail, necklace) and the unfamiliar (ostrich, octopus, owl). The whole thing is well put together, with each page full of detail without ever seeming cluttered.

What's Inside? The Alphabet Book
Satoshi Kitamura (illustrator)
Andersen Press (pb)

This is an alphabet book like no other. Starting with two packing cases labelled "a" and "b", a turn of a page reveals they are full of apples and bananas. But there is also a large dustbin on the same page, labelled "c" and "d" with something black sticking out of the top. Turn the page again, and this is shown to be part of a cat that has now climbed to the top of a lamp-post, leaving behind a ferocious dog. And so it goes on, with some of the word couplings becoming more and more odd as the book progresses (quill and rat, or woodpecker and xylophone). But Satoshi Kitamura is such a delightfully unpredictable artist that children will soon learn that although almost anything can happen on these pages what remains constant is the humour. "Guitar and Hippopotamus", for example, shows this huge animal surrounded by musical instruments singing to his own accompaniment. The box labelled "i" and "j" that he is sitting on shows enough of the iguana about to leap out on the following page to prepare the reader for what is going to happen and so let them in on the joke before it actually occurs. With so much else going on in terms of detail to seek out, abrupt changes of scenery and a

stream of illustrative jokes, this is a book to return to
long after the alphabet has been mastered simply for
the pleasure of its unique blend of artistry, imagination
and humour.

18 months to 2¹/2

Word Books

Children learn speech best both by listening to others and by being encouraged to speak for themselves. Parents and older helpers have been doing this last job ever since the human race began, talking to babies in deliberately slow, repetitive terms while encouraging anything the baby says in return often by turning it into a form of simplified speech. "Babytalk", the cut-down or made-up words that emerge in this way, is found in every culture.

When babies do start to learn speech, progress can be very rapid. Word books have been around for some time now, in order to cater for this early stage of vocabulary development. But while infants may learn some new words this way, the function of such books is more to enable children to practise words whose objects they already know from their daily experience. Those things which they do not recognize from real life and daily conversation will, on the whole, mean less to them, although there are always exceptions, particularly so in the case of exotic wild animals or dinosaurs known from books and films.

It is important, therefore, to use word books to consolidate experience as well as a way of breaking new ground. If a young child does react positively to an unfamiliar word or picture, well and good. But it is not the best idea to use wordbooks in an attempt either to teach or – even worse – to test at this stage, unless a child actually demands to be quizzed on how much he or she might recognize from the page. Adults with a mission to teach even the smallest of infants in anything like a formal classroom manner may be making a mistake. They will of course have already been teaching their babies in a far more informal manner often without realizing it. This instinctive type of teaching is usually conducted through the various dialogues parents and babies share as soon infants start babbling. Later on such dialogues become more verbalized on both sides, and some of these could well be further stimulated by word books – or indeed by any other sort of book. Attempts at more structured, deliberate teaching is best left until infants are much older.

The Baby's Catalogue
Allan Ahlberg (author)
Janet Ahlberg (illustrator)
Viking (hb) Puffin Books (pb)

Despite its title, Janet Ahlberg's ingeniously detailed pictures are on the whole more appropriate for infants past the baby stage. It is based on the whole notion of difference in family life, always an interesting idea for toddlers convinced that whatever they and their families do must not only be right but also widely imitated everywhere else. This book makes it clear from the outset that there are many different sorts of babies, with samples drawn from five fictional families displayed on the first page. The same is true of the five different mums and dads pictured, not to mention the five different types of high chairs, prams and swings, baths and bedtimes. Other daily events, objects and personalities that most toddlers will by now be familiar with are also pictured here in their full variety.

This sense of difference, both bewildering and fascinating for most toddlers, is beautifully captured in the affectionately realistic illustrations that appear in this picture book, already a classic for its age group. Toddlers are seen sleeping, crying and feeding as well as smiling; one mum has breakfast in her curlers while her smarter neighbour goes off to work in city clothes. Prams range from the stately to tiny models for transporting stuffed toys, and games go from catching and climbing to riding piggyback on an obliging dad. There is even a double page spread showing different types of accidents, though always featuring funny rather than dangerous examples. Allan Ahlberg and his wife Janet worked for years as a pair producing literature of rare quality for children of all ages. Their work is always recognizable for the quality and occasional unpredictability of its imagination, and never more so than in this gem of a book.

Ian Beck's Blue Book:
First words and pictures

Ian Beck (illustrator)

Scholastic Press (hb)

The same jolly, bushy-haired child, who could be a girl or boy, turns up in every page of this delightful board book. In the first picture the child gazes out of the window of "house" before going on to fly an "aeroplane" in the second. Other highlighted words include "cow", shown here jumping over the moon – a reference that small children should be able to recognize from their knowledge of nursery rhymes. The final picture of "bed" is typical of Ian Beck's general inventiveness. The cot in question is perched at the top of a tree clipped into a curious shape consisting of three separate levels. To get to it, the child in the picture has first to climb a long ladder – an idea more appealing in the imagination than in real life, at least where parents are concerned. Other illustrations are similarly full of incidental detail of the type that only

Ian Beck's
BLUE
BOOK
First words for baby

becomes obvious after repeated readings, such as the wind blowing the curtains out of the windows on page one. Word books for children sometimes try to cram in too much at a time; this one concentrates on quality rather than quantity and is all the better for it.

My First Word Book
Angela Wilkes (editor)
Dorling Kindersley (hb)

There are over one thousand photographs and illustrations in this book, starting with a section called "All about me" (face and body, including bottom and tummy button) then going on to "Cars", "At the Seaside" and "Colours, Shapes and Numbers". There is

18 months to 2½

also an attempt to explain some popular action words, which include sitting and lying down, and some position words, such as above, below and between. A few important storybook words are illustrated as well, among others a beaming young king and queen along with a witch, wizard and giant. The illustrations contain numerous, attractive photographs of actual children as well as simplified drawings in colour. Photographs of reality sometimes confuse children by showing them too much detail, but the drawings here reveal the essence of what they are describing by avoiding any tendency towards over-elaboration.

The editor makes some suggestions on how to use this book, including practising the 45 high-frequency words recorded on the opening page ("this", "they", "come", "the" and so on). But as these are exactly the sort of words parents use anyhow, there is no real need to incorporate them into specially constructed sentences as is suggested here. The book also advises parents to point to the simple word label underneath each picture as its name is pronounced. Again, there is no harm in this, but if children want to point at these lively pictures for quite different reasons – such as commenting on them or drawing attention to similar objects at home, this is just as good a way of using this well-designed and very popular book. Having sold over a million and a half copies since it first came out in 1991, this title seems set to stay around for a long time yet.

Stories

Enjoyment in books at this age is as before closely linked to the pleasures of close physical contact with whichever adult is doing the reading. Picking up a book by themselves and managing to turn the pages is not on the whole a skill that many children at this age range will possess for themselves. But seated next to an adult or else perched on a lap, infants quickly learn to recognize characters and objects in picture books, particularly when older readers point to details on the page while putting the sort of questions most infants can answer without too much trouble. As always, it is essential for adults to go with the flow where an infant's interest is concerned. If any particular book fails to appeal, never insist in presenting it, however well such a book might have been received elsewhere. All is not lost; a once unpopular book can sometimes turn into a favourite as an infant grows older. By the same token, if another book which seems less good is a success with a young reader, let them go on enjoying it.

Particular favourites at this age can be those books where children learn how to join in a regular refrain, whether this be a rhyme, a line of prose or just a collection of various farmyard imitations. Unfavourite books are less easy to predict, but should a child suddenly show distress at a picture – even if it looks quite harmless – learn from the child and put the book away for a future time. Most of us can remember a book or simply an illustration that once gave rise to strong, negative emotions when we were very young. Adults and older children can sometimes find such apparently out-of-scale responses quite amusing, but there is nothing funny in it as far as the infant is concerned. Potentially fearful books have their place only when small children are ready to take on their fears and, by so doing, defeat them at the same time. There are plenty of years for this to happen, and for the moment books like the titles selected below should simply serve as a source of interest and delight for small children and nothing else.

The Bear Went Over the Mountain

John Prater (author/illustrator)
Bodley Head (hb) Red Fox (pb)

Baby Bear approaches what looks like a range of brightly coloured hills. To the accompaniment of lines taken from the well-known song featured in the title, he first climbs up and then over this mountain "to see what he could see". When he eventually descends, the other side of the same mountain is revealed as nothing less than Big Bear lying in bed. Baby Bear climbs back again, and they end up playing in an increasingly disordered muddle of sheets, pillows and duvets.

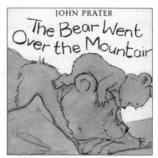

Most infants seem born with an irresistible impulse to climb over any known and loved adult body stretched out in front of them, whether in bed or anywhere else, and this story catches the physical intimacy shared between parent and child at those moments when everyone decides to play one last good game before finally getting up. John Prater has written and illustrated several board books about Baby Bear, all as happy and carefree as this one. A perfectionist who is adept at conveying feeling not just through expression but also from his characters' body language, his books are deserved best-sellers in an already overcrowded market of stories featuring bears big and small.

18 months to 2½

The Big Red Bus
Judy Hindley (author) **William Benedict** (illustrator)
Collins (pb)

18 months to 2¹/2

Children often seem to love buses as well as trains, which gives this engaging picture book something of a head start. The bus in question is a bright shade of red, also a colour popular with the young. When it runs into a hole in the road, a traffic jam quickly builds up composed of a van, car, motorbike, tipper truck and

steamroller. After that, a four page spread opens out, showing the whole line of waiting vehicles, their drivers now standing in the road talking to each other and wondering what to do. Finally a tractor pulls the red bus out of its hole, and every driver gets back into their vehicle – many infants will enjoy pointing out exactly who belongs to which form of transport long before anyone in the story has rejoined their vehicles. The hole is then repaired by the driver of the tipper truck assisted by the steamroller, driven in this case by a smart young lady in dungarees who also helps spread the burning tar. Traffic jams in real life are rarely as good-humoured as this, but infants won't mind. Instead, they will as always be fascinated by a glimpse into the adult world of who does what, particularly when they can see a normally male job performed here by a young woman. The text itself keeps to a minimum of words, but those that are included come out in giant speech bubbles, particularly "STOP!", always a useful word for the young to learn to recognize as early as possible.

Cock-a-Moo-Moo
Juliet Dallas-Conté (author) **Alison Bartlett** (illustrator)
Macmillan (hb)

Parents have been imitating animal noises to infants for centuries, with mimics in each nation sometimes choosing quite different words to imitate the same animal sounds (the French version of "cluck, cluck", for example, is "cot-cot-codec"). Some of the first items of speech in a human infant could well be their own reproduction of a particular favourite farmyard imitation. But in this picture book, the cockerel forgets his own cry and comes out with those of other animals instead. This gives everyone a chance to correct him, and parents who pride themselves on their own range of animal noises will have a fine time imitating them all here, both those that the cockerel gets wrong and those of the affronted animals whose cries he seems to be taking over. Hugely colourful pictures accompany this story, which should prove a riot when read aloud in the privacy of the home (reading it with similar gusto to an infant on a crowded train is probably not recommended).

Dear Zoo
Rod Campbell (author/illustrator)
Campbell Books (hb) Puffin Books (pb)

Any book devised and illustrated by Rod Campbell is worth looking out for. While other author/ illustrators may be happy to repeat the same old formula,

Campbell is always on the lookout for something different. This freshness of vision has been justifiably rewarded by high sales combined with critical success. In this particular title, for example, each page contains a flap hiding an animal that has been sent to the child narrator by the zoo as a pet. What is new is that each flap is designed to look like a different form of packaging, ranging from a yellow elephant crate, labelled "Very Heavy", to a basket for a snake and a red, wooden box with a grill for a lion. None of these animals is named as such; children are instead invited to identify them each time their particular container is opened. Lift-the-flap books may not always enjoy a long life with infants, with the flaps themselves often working loose or eventually tearing off. But the pleasure they give during their sometimes short life can still be enormous, and never more so than in this particular title here.

Eat Your Peas

Kes Gray (author) **Nick Sharratt** (illustrator)
Bodley Head (hb) Red Fox (pb)

Mum tells Daisy to eat up her peas, but without success. On each page after that she adds a further bribe, starting with ice cream, going on to an offer of staying up for an extra half-hour before promising no less than 100 puddings, ten new bikes and a personal chocolate factory for good measure. Each new bribe is pictured on the page at the moment it is made, but Daisy still has the last word and the peas remain defiantly uneaten.

This is an excellent example of an accumulative story, where each new event or object is shown joining an increasingly long list of what has already gone before. For toddlers, such stories also operate as good memory tests, giving them the chance to repeat the refrain as it returns over and over again. This book adds in generous amounts of humour through Nick Sharratt's illustrations. Each picture shows Daisy in greater close-up, ending with a huge face gazing out at readers. Detail is kept to a minimum, which is just as well given that mum's final promises include the whole of Africa, space rockets, the earth, the moon, the stars and the sun. At this stage, this accumulative story turns into another favourite genre with small children: the tall story, so exaggerated

that in the end nobody can believe it, even inexperienced readers. But they can still laugh at such exaggerations, as they surely will here – particularly when all these impossibilities are illustrated so vividly.

Ginger
Charlotte Voake (author/illustrator)
Walker Books (hb & pb)

Charlotte Voake is a fine artist, equally at home in colour or black-and-white, and in this book, she combines ink and watercolours to create two totally convincing cats. Ginger is old and settled, used to his daily routine with the small girl who takes such good care of him. But when she introduces a pushy young kitten, nothing is the same again. Infants following this story may have their own feelings about intruders within the family, should there be a new baby around at the time. Others, possibly with older siblings, might feel more sympathy for the kitten, who is up against such an immovable, superior presence. Ginger finally resolves to leave the house, a picture of injured dignity as he passes through the cat flap out into the garden. He is quickly found, though, and after some diplomatic intervention from the little girl both animals finally make friends. In this simple story, told with a minimum of words printed in a large typeface, the pictures are so tactile it is sometimes difficult to remember not to stroke the cats from one page to another. A worthy winner of several prizes, this is a perfect book for any young reader, pet-loving or not.

Handa's Surprise

Eileen Browne (author/illustrator)

Mantra Publishing (hb) Walker Books (pb)

This is another story about a walk where everything happens behind the unknowing pedestrian's back. With illustrations based on children from the Luo tribe of Southwest Kenya, it conveys all the warmth of a very hot country. Setting out for a neighbouring village, Handa fills her basket with exotic fruit to give to her friend Akeyo. As each page turns, a wild animal steals something from the straw basket perched on Handa's head. But a chance encounter with some falling tangerines somewhat restores the situation, leaving everyone thoroughly contented. Children who only know bananas, mangos and pineapples from the shelves of supermarkets may be interested to see where all this fruit actually comes from. They should also enjoy a glimpse of a traditional, working African village, with babies carried on backs and domestic animals wandering about at will. Throw in popular wild beasts like elephants and zebras, and here surely is a book for every child to enjoy.

Hello Lulu
Caroline Uff (author/illustrator)
Orchard Books (hb & pb)

Very little happens in this charming picture book, but this leaves more for infants to add in for themselves. Starting with the little girl's house, there are glimpses of the family car, parents, a brother and sister, a favourite toy, some clothes, pets, a best friend and some food. Each picture is huge, simple and affectionate, with clear pastel colours and big smiles all round. The first time an infant goes through this book, he or she will simply be interested in what

Lulu possesses for herself. But in subsequent readings, there is an obvious invitation for young readers to supply their own answers to such basic questions as where is your Mummy and Daddy? What do you most like to eat? What's your brother and sister called? Simple books can in this way often provoke quite complex answers from infants, so long as there is someone to pose the questions and then be there to listen to the answers, helping out when needed. It is hard to think of a happier picture book than this one; it may well need its special, extra sturdy pages, given the amount of attention and use it seems likely to get.

I Want My Potty

Tony Ross (author/illustrator)

Andersen Press (hb)

HarperCollins (pb)

In this story, a little princess starts by deciding that potties are not really the thing at all, despite getting fed up with her wet nappies. Eventually her mother persuades her otherwise, and after a

few mishaps, vividly portrayed here, potty and princess become the closest of friends. But one day, when she most needs her favourite object, it fails to reach her in time. This is despite the combined efforts of king, cook, maid, gardener, general and finally an admiral, who has secretly added the potty to his fleet of toy boats floating in the sea. There are no recriminations about the puddle that results, and everyone will surely enjoy this exceptionally good-humoured story. Princess, Queen and King are depicted as a thoroughly ordinary family except for their cardboard gold crowns. But the illusion of grandeur is still there, and Tony Ross's pictures are witty in the extreme; the picture of the princess straining to perform while courtiers look on worriedly should make anyone laugh.

It's Mine
Rod Campbell (author/illustrator)
Campbell Books (hb & pb)

At some stage small children have to learn how to recognize objects just from a few visual clues rather than by seeing an entire object. Picture books have always been useful during this particular period of growth, often turning such interpretive sleuthing into a game. In this little board book, each different animal (which appears in full on the following page) is anticipated only

18 months to 2 1/2

by a small detail. Thus, a pink tongue, on turning the page, is seen to belong to a jovial looking tiger. And so it continues, with one major surprise reserved for the end: when children start thinking they have finally cracked the code, a splendid lion appears whose mouth opens as the page is turned. There is no warning or anticipation beforehand, but most children find such surprises exciting as well as fun.

Katy Cat and Beaky Boo

Lucy Cousins (author/illustrator)

Walker Books (hb & pb)

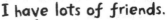

I have lots of friends.

There are over forty flaps in this book, covering different colours, textures, noises, clothes, foods, dwelling places and numbers. Beaky Boo is the bird to whom Katy Cat puts all her questions, but the answers – which reveal themselves as each flap is lifted – are designed to come from infants themselves. There is no story as such, but Lucy Cousins draws with a firm line and an eye for attractive detail, and the vivid splashes of colour as well as the differently shaped flaps (long for a snake, tiny for a mouse) all help to build up an atmosphere of fun. This is a truly interactive book which gives children the task of first lifting the flaps and then describing what they see beneath. For those times when the desire to perform is there plus an adult audience eager to join in, then this could be just the book required.

Mr Gumpy's Outing

John Burningham (author/illustrator)

Jonathan Cape (hb) Red Fox (pb)

The story is simple enough: good-natured Mr Gumpy sets out on a river trip in his flat-bottomed boat. On the way he picks up various children and animals, first making them promise to behave. But for all their good intentions, mayhem eventually breaks out. The boat sinks, but when everyone has swum to the shore Mr Gumpy marches

18 months to 2¹/₂

them away to tea, all forgiven. What makes this book truly outstanding – and one reason why it won the Kate Greenaway Award in 1970 – is its dazzling mixture of artistic techniques: ink drawings on the left-hand side contrast with colour wash, crayon, pastels plus the occasional use of cellulose and gouache on the right.

John Burningham, half in humour, once said that "An artist is crippled in this country by the reproductions of his work, so I put a lot into my drawings, knowing I'll be left with something." Such diversity of graphic techniques certainly works in this story, where child-like shapes are made magical by the use of swirling lines and different, dappled colours. Translated into eleven different languages, Burningham's picture books constantly break new artistic ground while always staying close to an infant's emotions and imagination. Reading this particular story has much of the pleasure of going out on a real picnic in the countryside, with the sun beating down on unfamiliar but beautiful scenery.

On Your Potty!

Virginia Miller (author/illustrator)

Walker Books (hb & pb)

Potties, for so long taboo objects in children's books, are now almost as familiar in illustrations aimed at the young as they are in a toddler's bedroom. How parents react to books about them will depend in part on their own attitudes to potty-training at home. In this book, produced on tough, thickened pages, Bartholomew Bear is made to feel somewhat guilty when, having refused the chance before, he suddenly gets caught short when playing outside. But by running as fast as he can he reaches his potty just in time, and is then rewarded by a big hug. This is just one book about this small, cuddly character; other typically directive titles from the same author-illustrator include *Be Gentle!*, *Get Into Bed!*, *Eat Your Dinner!* and *In a Minute!* The pictures themselves are always great fun, with Bartholomew shown as particularly good at sticking up for himself before finally deciding to obey house rules.

18 months to 2½

Rosie's Walk
Pat Hutchins (author/illustrator)
Bodley Head (hb) Red Fox (pb)

There are only 32 words of text in this famous picture book, now a best-seller for over three decades. Most of the story is told by the illustrations alone, leaving children with the delightful task of piecing it all together and perhaps ending up retelling the whole plot to themselves. All the main features of the story, except for the fox itself, can be seen on the inside cover, which

pictures a farmyard and its surroundings in glowing colours. The animals and their surrounding rural scenery are depicted in stylized, static shapes, not unlike folk art or some of the painted toys small children are likely to be familiar with. When Rosie the hen does set out she is followed by a fox who is highly visible to readers but not to her. But each attempted leap on to its prey is foiled as the fox first steps on a rake, later plunges into an unseen pool and is finally chased away by a swarm of bees.

Being in the position of knowing better than others does not often fall to small readers, so it is hardly surprising that they enjoy this story so much. Rosie's blithe indifference to the danger facing her raises much the same reactions that also cause children to shout out "He's *behind* you!" at the pantomime. The various reasons why the fox misses each time start as simple to work out and end up rather more complex, but infants should find it easy to put cause and effect together in their own minds from the generous clues given to them throughout this picture book. This is just one of the many ways in which following a story in pictures can also become an exercise in learning how to think logically. The fact that such an exercise is also deeply enjoyable renders any accompanying learning all the more fun.

Tiny Rabbit Goes to the Park
John Wallace (author/illustrator)
Viking (hb) Puffin Books (pb)

This is another picture book where nothing very much happens but which also gets close to some of a small child's chief preoccupations. Rabbit decides to go to the park, taking with him his own favourite stuffed toy bunny. Since Rabbit looks like a toy himself, the idea of a toy possessing its own smaller toy is in itself quite an interesting notion for infants to chew over. After playing for a while with other animal friends, Rabbit discovers that his bunny has disappeared – the sort of loss that many children will have experienced for themselves. Stories often prompt thoughts or questions about other similar events at this age, leading at times to quite protracted discussions in the middle of any particular tale. This sometimes turns reading to a small child into quite a drawn-out affair, but the rewards can be great too. It has always been known that stories feed the imagination, but what is sometimes overlooked is

18 months to 2 1/2

the way they also stimulate speech, especially in very young readers eager to make sense not just of what they are reading but also what they can remember elsewhere as the story progresses.

Toffee Takes a Nap
Sally Chambers (author/illustrator)
Piccadilly Press (pb)

Small children usually adore pets, imagining them at times to possess various human attributes including the powers of speech. But they also know that animals are different from people, and it is this particular quality of same-different that helps make stories about pets so interesting to them. In this picture book, Toffee – so called because of her brown coat – is very much a cat rather than a human in disguise. She goes to sleep, rolls over into a garden pond, and then looks for somewhere quiet to dry off. Noisy birds disturb her, but Toffee is not shown to be interested in killing – like most fictional cats, she comes over as extremely positive towards wild life. Telling the whole truth to children about animals, including details of their aggressive tendencies, generally has to wait until readers are much older. Even so, there is still a fairly realistic cat fight here, with Toffee finally running away into the house to her favourite position of all: squatting down on the artist's own desk in the middle of pens, pencils, rulers and unfinished work. Children often think that picture books simply appear as if by magic. Showing them an illustration of one still at an unfinished state provides an interesting extra touch in a picture book that already has a lot going for it.

The Train Ride
June Crebbin (author) **Stephen Lambert** (illustrator)
Walker Books (pb)

Steam trains always seem popular with small readers, even those who have never actually travelled in one. This story cleverly reproduces in its simple verses the insistent beat of such a train as it speeds along. Big, pastel pictures show sheep, cows, tractors and geese in the fields as the engine goes hurtling by, and entering a dark tunnel halfway along provides yet another excitement. The train itself, bright red and puffing out

18 months to 2½

white smoke, is closer to a toy than the real thing, as are its smiling driver and ticket collector. But when the little girl and her mother featured in the story finally arrive at a small seaside station, a very human-looking grandmother is there to give them both a warm welcome. One day children will discover that rail travel in Britain is seldom quite as pleasurable as this, but for the moment they can and should revel in the romantic possibilities of taking a journey where there is always something interesting to look out for through the window, and where the train itself, spotless and highly coloured, seems as anxious to join in the fun as everyone else.

The Very Hungry Caterpillar
Eric Carle (author/illustrator)
Hamish Hamilton (hb) Puffin Books (pb)

There are no flaps in this famous book, but plenty of holes made by the hungry caterpillar as he eats his way from one object to another. Translated into thirty languages, it is easy to see why this title should have become such a phenomenal success, with sales at the latest count numbering over fourteen million. Picture books that deviated from the norm were comparatively rare in 1970, when this work first came out. But because infants can actually feel as well as see the holes

the caterpillar is making, in what was then a novel effect, the whole story becomes that much more real. Almost as important are the colours and sheer scale of this book. Leaves seem greener, the sun more yellow and the strawberries redder than in real life, and all looking quite vast at the same time. The final moment, when the caterpillar is shown stretched across two full pages in his new guise as a fully grown butterfly, is so bright as to catch the breath the first time any toddler gets to it. Eric Carle has produced over seventy picture books, some containing other surprises (*The Very Quiet Cricket*, for example, contains a device that makes a cricket-type noise at the opening of the last page). But *The Very Hungry Caterpillar* is still his masterpiece, and it's worth investing in the hardback edition for its sheer, eye-popping scale.

18 months to 2½

Where's Spot?
Eric Hill (author/illustrator)
Frederick Warne (hb) Puffin Books (pb)

Spot is a puppy who has temporarily disappeared. His
mother goes round the house looking for him in all the
possible places, and each new search entails raising a
flap on a different page – the joke being that every one
of these flaps conceals something totally unexpected,
including a bear, a snake, a lion and a crocodile. Spot's
mother remains supremely untroubled by any of these
apparitions, and so too will infants, since this is
obviously a book designed to please rather than scare,
while the final joyous reunion of mother and puppy
has all the warmth of any child re-united with his or
her own mother. Even so, lifting up flaps here has an
edge of excitement and surprise as well, making this
one of those stories which, when first encountered,
often has to be read again and again until infants know

exactly what is going to happen.
Searching for others hiding
from them is a standard part
of play for all children,
with games of hide-
and-seek in
picture
books
often almost as
much fun as
the real thing.

Another Ten Spot Books

Spot Goes to the Farm
Spot's Baby Sister
Spot Goes to the Circus
Spot Stays Overnight
Spot Bakes a Cake

Spot Goes to the Park
Spot's First Christmas
Spot Goes to School
Spot Goes on Holiday
Spot's First Walk

18 months to 2¹/₂

Older toddlers

$2^1/_2$ to $3^1/_2$

Older toddlers

$2^{1/2}$ to $3^{1/2}$

While children of this age group remain interested in depictions in books of their everyday existence and general surroundings, they are now also more able to start exploring tales that leave the immediate here and now in favour of something more imaginative. Favourite books at this age often represent a mixture of the comparatively mundane and the out-of-this-world. Pets in stories, for example, either behave like dumb animals or else appear as surrogate human beings complete with speech, clothes and their own houses. Similarly, toys in books may be there simply to be played with or else are shown with an ability to think for themselves.

All the books recommended in this section are illustrated, but pictures can now afford to be more
sophisticated, often using a greater abundance of detail
and going in for more complex and stylized shapes.
Adults can always help in identifying relevant detail in
illustrations in the course of reading out whatever story
is involved, but children in their own turn might notice
things themselves that a parent may have missed.
Whatever the reaction to any particular picture book
though, it is unlikely ever to be final. Readers of any age
often think of other things as well in the course of reading or listening to a story. Now that infants are
developing their own powers of speech, those reading
to them can therefore expect numbers of questions and
observations as the story progresses. One page may
remind a child of an equivalent happening in their own
life, which must of course be related immediately to
whoever is reading the story. Another page may give
rise to questions about what has just happened before
in the story, what exactly is happening now and what
might happen in the immediate future. Reading stories
to infants is rarely an uninterrupted business, except
perhaps with books so well-known that there is hardly
anything left to say about them.

As with all ages, certain stories relate directly to a
child's own emotional experiences. Numbers of modern
stories, for example, follow traditional fairy tales by

2¹/₂ to 3¹/₂

describing scenes of sibling rivalry, jealous possessiveness, the desire of the small to triumph over bigger people and other situations not unknown to children in ordinary family life. If a child is having a particular problem, reading a story where the hero or heroine is going through the same sort of thing and seeing how it is all eventually resolved could prove relieving as well as satisfying. But it is not on the whole a good idea to introduce books to small children only with the idea that these might do them some psychological good. It is far better to choose stories that infants seem to enjoy, given that such pleasure may in itself be an indication that the book is responding to a psychological need while providing entertainment at the same time.

2½ to 3½

Stories

2¹/₂ to 3¹/₂

Stories for this age have to be fairly short and simple. The vocabulary used should not include too many difficult words, and there should always be the possibility of a certain amount of repetition. Characters involved will often be those already most familiar to readers in real life, such as parents, grandparents, brothers and sisters. The most common mode of stories will be humour, usually arising from simple mistakes or misapprehensions. There is room however for drama too, sometimes revolving around young characters trying to come to terms with their own occasional capacity for anger and aggression. Such anger can by symbolized in a variety of ways, with illustrations playing their own part when it comes to creating the monsters or wild animals so useful for symbolizing a child's own internal state of aggression. But such creatures must not be too terrifying. It is important that young readers are always left feeling that they, or those characters representing them, are the ones who are left finally in charge and on top.

Small children have short concentration spans, and they particularly like stories that end on a high note with lots of movement and energy, reflecting perhaps their own occasional need to let off steam after listening to a story quietly. The glimpses they get in illustrations for stories of the outside world tend to be more idealized than realistic, often showing town or country landscapes at their most attractive. Main characters themselves, however, often look grotesque, drawn with a cartoonist's eye for exaggeration. Such characters, whether human or animal, are excellent for expressing the various over-the-top emotions that children can now recognize in others from their own experience of such feelings themselves. The fact that characters are so often drawn in cartoon shape means that small children can both identify with them and at the same time keep their distance should the story in which they feature ever look for a moment as if it might be spinning out of control.

2¹/₂ to 3¹/₂

The Biggest Bed in the World
Lindsay Camp (author) **Jonathan Langley** (illustrator)
Collins (pb)

This story is about that most contentious of subjects where many small children and parents are concerned: who sleeps in whose bed. It begins with Mum, Dad and baby Ben, all just about able to share a double bed until Ben grows too big and starts wriggling. Dad keeps building bigger beds thereafter, but new additions to his family continue to crowd him out as before. Having finally dismantled the top of his house in order to install the biggest bed in the world, Dad still finds that everyone is conspiring against him and his need for sleep. Things end happily enough, though, and children as well as parents will surely be amused by a situation most of them will recognize from their own lives. There is so much else to look at here as well: Mum feeding one of the new babies, floors littered with toys and pets and a few glimpses outside of idyllic seaside scenes. For parents who are still not getting good nights on a regular basis,

2½ to 3½

this book also offers quite a useful peg for discussion
with any of their own children who might still be
raiding the parental bed after dark.

Clever Bill
William Nicholson (author/illustrator)
Heinemann (hb)

Sir William Nicholson was a famous artist whose
forceful images brought a completely new look to
illustration at the end of the nineteenth century. In
1926 he produced this classic picture book, which has
been a favourite with children ever since. His
illustrations have all the roughness and immediacy of

2½ to 3½

artwork that has just been produced: heavy black lines frame each page, with handwritten captions running underneath. The story itself, about a little girl packing her case and forgetting her favourite toy, is pleasant if unremarkable. What makes this book so special is the way it conjures up a lost world of old-fashioned toys, clothes and steam trains while making them seem completely fresh at the same time. As in all the best picture books, story and text act as one, sometimes invading each other's territory but always working together. Picture books have always had the power to offer vivid glimpses not just of contemporary scenes and people but also of worlds that have gone. This story does so in a way that is always memorable, while maintaining the highest artistic standards.

Dad! I Can't Sleep

Michael Foreman (author/illustrator)

Red Fox (pb)

Little Panda cannot get to sleep, so Dad offers advice. Count sheep, he suggests, and when that fails to work he substitutes cows, pigs, tigers, elephants and even dinosaurs – but all without effect. As each suggestion is made, the animal forms itself in Little Panda's imagination and is then pictured flying across the bedroom ceiling. When Dad finally goes upstairs in exasperation he opens the door onto a giant, fold-out picture. This shows his son's room crowded with all the various animals conjured up, each one now wanting its own drink.

Children will already know quite a lot about the powers of the imagination, and will appreciate the way in which verbal suggestions are turned into real pictures. They also have experience at calling parents up to them after going to bed, and may enjoy the spectacle of someone else their age trying this on for themselves. Best of all for them, perhaps, is the moment when diplodocuses, stegosauruses and pterodactyls join the weird procession passing over Little Panda's ceiling. Infants often have a soft spot for dinosaurs, and these manage to come over here as almost cuddly. Elsewhere, the stars and elephants on Little Panda's bedding and the moon lampshade on his bedside light make their way later into the pictures of his imagination. Downstairs, a photograph on the wall shows dad weight-lifting while in the foreground he is seen trying

2¹/₂ to 3¹/₂

to get on with the family ironing. Every detail here is made to count, so that there is always much else to look out for in this delightful story.

Duck in the Truck
Jez Alborough (author/illustrator)
HarperCollins (hb & pb)

In fact Duck doesn't get very far in this lively, rhyming story once his truck gets stuck in the muck. A sheep in a jeep and a goat in a boat help out, and all ends happily – for the duck at least. There are so many things children will enjoy here: the duck's bright red car, the rich brown mud where he gets trapped and the final heave when everyone falls over. Set amidst rural scenery that appears to stretch far into the distance, this is a story to return to again and again. Its verse couplets, though never great poetry, have a pleasing rhythm plus an ability to stick in the mind even after just a few repetitions.

The Elephant and the Bad Baby
Elfrida Vipont (author) **Raymond Briggs** (illustrator)
Puffin (pb)

This classic book, first published in 1969, combines an

2½ to 3½

excellent accumulative story with a superb set of illustrations. When author and illustrator work separately, close co-operation between the two can sometimes prove difficult, which is why it is single author-illustrators who often produce the best picture books. But these pages show two collaborators perfectly complementing what the other is doing. The story is close to the sort of dream where normal rules get broken in the most satisfying way. A small toddler meets a massive elephant, and together they set off pilfering from whatever shop they are passing at the time. The refrain "Rumpeta, rumpeta, rumpeta" beats out each time as the elephant and his naughty friend charge along, followed by an ever-growing line of angry shopkeepers. Colour on the left-hand pages is balanced by black and white on the right. But just when the baby has got almost everything he wants, he is dumped by the elephant for the crime of never saying "Please". He immediately does so, but also asks to be taken back to his mother as well.

However much children enjoy the spectacle of someone their own age behaving badly and getting away with it, there is also the wish to see normal rules more or less restored by the last page. This is exactly what happens in this story, so allowing toddlers to have it both ways – relishing the mayhem the baby brings but also sharing in the final disapproval of someone who always wants to have things his own way without showing any gratitude. They will also understand that after an exciting adventure it is nice to be able to return to home and security. To this ancient balance between order and disorder is added the humour of Raymond Briggs's unique style of illustration. While the shopkeepers are shown as angry for most of the time (but also forgiving and understanding when it really matters), each of them is endowed with a distinct character. Parents who enjoyed this book themselves when young will be pleased to know that it's still also going strong today, ready for a fresh generation interested in running away with an elephant in the safety of their imagination. If it also succeeds in teaching them the value of saying "Please", then so much the better.

2½ to 3½

Ellie's Growl

Karen Popham (author/illustrator)

Frances Lincoln (hb & pb)

Ellie's older brother William is very good at making animal noises during reading sessions with her. But when Ellie decides to imitate his terrible growl, she upsets both her dog and a little boy at the swings. Her kitten is made of stronger stuff, though, growling back so fiercely that Ellie decides in future it's better to purr instead. This magical picture book brings different animals to life at the moment when William imitates them, so that at various moments the bathroom fills up with sea lions and the bedroom is crammed with whinnying zebras, slithering snakes and chest-beating baboons. Knowing that these animals only exist in Ellie's imagination allows Karen Popham to exhibit her best illustrative effects, producing a truly ferocious tiger and some furiously flapping swans. Children will know from their own experience the way they can imagine the different characters they hear about in stories, and in this book they see such fantasies brought thrillingly to life. It also allows parents a good opportunity to talk about the experience of reading books in general, asking their own children what other pictures they may sometimes be making up for themselves when they are listening to stories. Informal discussions of or around favourite books – when young readers are in the mood

2¹/₂ to 3¹/₂

– can sometimes open up a rich vein of conversation between parent and child. But such discussion should never be forced, and on the whole are best left for times when everyone involved seems equally interested and there is no pressure for any "right" answers or responses.

Elmer
David McKee (author/illustrator)
Andersen Press (hb) Red Fox (pb)

Elmer is an elephant who also happens to be a born a bright patchwork of colours. The other elephants enjoy this, but Elmer gets tired of his unwanted fame and decides to rub himself down with some grey berries in order to look like a normal elephant. A shower of rain – and his own lively sense of

2¹/₂ to 3¹/₂

humour – then sees him return to his former patchwork glory. But this time the other elephants agree to decorate themselves once a year while on the same day Elmer can revert to grey once again. Not the greatest of stories, perhaps, but the sensational illustrations for this book make up for it. It's more than possible that Elmer is the brightest thing a child will ever have seen – until the moment at the end of the story when all the other elephants burst into colour as well.

Small children learn a great deal from picture books as they mature, relishing the opportunity to gaze at static pages which are so much easier to concentrate on than the moving objects of a television screen. In this story they can see how some shapes remain constant even when colours change – an important step forwards in making sense of the physical world around them. And at another level, they can learn something about the value of staying individual even when pressure to join the rest of the crowd is intense.

2¹/₂ to 3¹/₂

Some More Elmer Books

Elmer Again

Elmer on Stilts

Elmer and Wilbur

Elmer in the Snow

Elmer and the Wind

Elmer and the
Lost Teddy

Elmer's Concert

Fox's New Coat

Jonathan Emmett (author) **Penny Ives** (illustrator)

Viking (hb) Puffin (pb)

Foxes have a reputation for cunning in children's stories, so it makes a nice change to find one in this book who is more gullible than all the other animals around her. In this story, a lady fox buys a beautiful woollen coat, only to have it unravel page after page so that she finally ends up with a big ball of multicoloured wool and not much else. Fortunately, the other animal club together to knit her a new one, so everything ends happily. The process of unravelling starts almost immediately, so that infants can follow the various trailing

2½ to 3½

126

threads from page to page. They can also see what the fox cannot: the slow disintegration of a once-perfect garment. All the other animals know it too and do their best to warn her about what is happening, and this state of knowing best can also be greatly enjoyed by all young readers. Brightly illustrated, this book pictures a dreamworld where animals talk, dress in human clothes and remain perfectly friendly with each other. Such a vision of harmony between the various species is as old as stories about the Garden of Eden before the Fall, and is always particularly popular with small readers.

Giraffes Can't Dance
Giles Andreae (author) **Guy Parker-Rees** (illustrator)
Orchard Books (hb & pb)

The author wrote this book after a trip to Kenya where he was particularly impressed by the elegance of the giraffes. The story is one more variant on the universal

Cinderella theme, where someone overlooked and despised goes on to become the envy of everyone else. Told in rhyming verse with a bouncy rhythm, the best moments take place in a final massive Jungle Dance held every year. Infants who like dancing themselves can only be inspired by the sight of the rock-and-rolling rhinos, the lions dancing a sexy tango, the chimps doing the cha-cha and the baboons who team up for a Scottish reel. In the background, the African jungle gleams and throbs with noise and colour. The author is also known as the successful contemporary poet Purple Ronnie while the illustrator, Guy Parker-Rees, is one of the most exciting young artists in the children's book world. Together they make a formidable team, and this picture book is a brilliant achievement.

Goodnight Moon

Margaret Wise Brown (author) **Clement Hurd** (illustrator)
Campbell Books (board)

First published in 1947, this magical book rapidly established itself as a children's classic. It is set in a brightly coloured bedroom where a baby rabbit lies in bed while an old lady rabbit sits knitting in a chair. Each page brings one of the details of this room into closer focus as the eyes of the baby rabbit – still not quite asleep – wander from one favourite object to

another. There are pictures on the wall, a pair of kittens
on the floor plus the usual bedroom collection of lights,
chairs and toys, each one of which is wished good night
before the old lady finally leaves the baby rabbit fast
asleep. In this last picture, all the objects so far picked
out are seen in their proper place, and yet this is far
more than just another book inviting children to use
their powers of observation and object recognition.
What stays in the memory, above all, is the mood of
security and tranquillity generated by Brown's simple
rhyming text and Clement Hurd's delightful pictures in
which glowing colours alternate with black, white and
grey, so preparing readers for the time when the light is
finally turned out for the rest of the night.

129

Humphrey's Corner

Sally Hunter (author/illustrator)

Puffin (pb)

2½ to 3½

Humphrey is a baby elephant, but in every other way he is a normal human child looking for somewhere interesting to play at home. He trails round the house with his "mooey" (a small comfort blanket) and Mop, his stuffed rabbit. Each room he visits is pictured from the point of view of someone not much over two feet tall. Doors tower, chairs have to be climbed up and stairs can only be managed with difficulty. This also has something to do with the fact that Humphrey is now wearing his mother's high-heeled shoes while trying at the same time to carry around a box which includes her sparkly necklace plus his favourite towel. Drawn with the softest of crayons, the book captures all the inconsequentiality of a child's aimless play until Mum takes a hand, suggesting he stays near her in the kitchen in his own favourite toy castle. Children with their own special corners at home will look on with sympathy as Humphrey tries to find his. They should also sense the loving affection with which these illustrations are drawn, and the way that Humphrey sees things from a point of view that is also their own. A number of other picture books about this baby elephant also exist, equally charming and worth looking out for.

Four More Humphrey Books

Humphrey's Christmas   Humphrey's Bedtime
Humphrey's Garden   Humphrey's Playtime

Inside Mary Elizabeth's House

Pamela Allen (author/illustrator)

Viking (hb)

On her way to school, Mary Elizabeth tells four rough boys that there's a monster in her house. They don't believe her even though he can clearly be seen, one foot sticking out of the chimney, another bursting out of a window. Mary herself is on good terms with the apparition and he enjoys her company too. Finally she asks the disbelieving boys back to tea, and has the great satisfaction of seeing them chased away by the monster at his most terrifying. He and Mary Elizabeth then return home, hand in hand.

Monsters don't get much shaggier or more menacing than this one, but because Mary Elizabeth sees him as a friend who helps her hold her own against some jeering older boys, young readers should take to him as well and perhaps realize that imaginary monsters – or those in picture books – can be more than aggressive fantasies. They can also, as here, have the role of defender of the weak, and are important as such. Unlike

2½ to 3½

Freud, the psychologist Carl Jung believed that the potential aggression and destructiveness associated with the unconscious was by no means all bad. While Freud taught that such feelings had to be totally repressed in order for civilization to become possible, Jung stated that they had their positive side too, not least as a store of energy which individuals could tap for their own purposes. This picture book, which seems to have the same sort of message, is illustrated by Pamela Allen with wit and style as well as with a sympathetic understanding. Although small and comparatively defenceless children know very well that they cannot summon up monsters to fight their battles for them, they can still do the next best thing and imagine a situation where this is possible, which is what this picture book is all about.

2½ to 3½

Little Bear's Trousers

Jane Hissey (author/illustrator)

Hutchinson (hb) Red Fox (pb)

This is just one of the many stories about Little Bear written and illustrated by Jane Hissey. Extraordinarily successful with young readers, they describe different days in the life of a toy bear surrounded by a fixed cast of other stuffed animals. Nothing very much happens, but it is a mistake to think that infants always want adventure and excitement in books. Placid stories have

their place too, especially when they are as artfully illustrated as here. Everything is seen from a small toy's point of view, with bathroom taps looming like steel chimneys and pudding bowls big enough to climb into. The various bizarre uses Little Bear's trousers are put to

2¹/₂ to 3¹/₂

before he finally retrieves them should also amuse young readers, accustomed as they will be to losing their own clothes on occasions.

Little Brother and the Cough

Hiawyn Oram (author) **Mary Rees** (illustrator)
Frances Lincoln (hb & pb)

This picture book is an ingenious study of child psychology but at a level which child readers as well as parents can readily understand. On the first day that her mother and father bring home a new baby brother, big sister of around three years old suddenly develops a bad cough. Not only can this cough be heard, it can also be seen, sitting above the little girl's head in a type of speech bubble. It looks just like the little girl too, except that while she appears only mildly grumpy, the cough's permanent expression is positively evil. When baby brother wants to sleep, the cough sounds worse than ever while dancing with rage above the little girl's head. And so it goes on, with the cough spoiling everything it can until finally it goes too far, suggesting

2½ to 3½

134

to the little girl that she rock her brother's pram until it tips over. Mother and father come to the rescue, making all the fuss of her that the little girl had been waiting for all the time. Happy and reassured at last, she is put to bed surrounded by her favourite toys while the cough packs her bag and departs through the window. The little girl is now shown finally making friends with her brother.

Everyone knows about the realities of sibling rivalry, particularly for a firstborn child who will never have realized what it was like to share his or her parents until another baby comes along. This story sets out to explain and then defuse this type of situation in a way that could be genuinely useful to any family currently going through the same experience. Children are not fools in these matters, though, and can resent heavy-handed attempts to offer advice and understanding.

2½ to 3½

135

This is where Mary Rees's illustrations make all the difference. Here is an illustrator whose adults, children and pets all look like rather amiable grotesques and such comic-strip characters further lighten a message already put over in an admirably deft and amusing way by the author Hiawyn Oram. Being funny is not necessarily the opposite of being serious; it can also be a way, as here, of putting over an important message in a manner both charming in itself and highly effective at the same time.

Meg and Mog

Helen Nicoll (author) **Jan Pienkowski** (illustrator)
Puffin (pb)

Given that the very idea of a witch often creates terror in small children, it may seem bizarre to create a whole picture book series about one. But a good way to take on fear has always been to confront

2¹/₂ to 3¹/₂

the object concerned and in doing so discover that in truth there is nothing to be frightened of at all. This is exactly what happens in this engaging picture book and all its many sequels. Meg the witch is first shown as an ordinary young woman asleep in bed. Waking up at midnight, she slowly gets dressed, allowing children to watch the gradual transformation of an adolescent girl into a beaming (and not at all scary) young witch. She and her cat Mog then have breakfast before flying up the chimney to join a party of other cheerful-looking witches, all shown having a great time at no inconvenience to anyone else. They eventually gather round a cauldron but the mixture goes wrong, turning all except Meg into mice.

However reassuring the text, much will depend on the illustrations when it comes to establishing an atmosphere children will find attractive as well as unthreatening. Jan Pienkowski achieves this here with the minimum of detail, creating the sort of witch that children could almost draw for themselves. The apparent simplicity, though, disguises a mastery of line and a skillful use of silhouette effects. Some past images of witches in picture books seemed designed to horrify a young audience, but there is no such intention in this book, with pictures matching text in offering small readers a really good time while also transforming former objects of fear into new imaginary playmates.

2¹/2 to 3¹/2

2½ to 3½

Peace At Last
Jill Murphy (author/illustrator)
Campbell Books (hb) Macmillan (pb)

Although Mrs Bear and Baby Bear have no problem
getting to sleep, Mr Bear cannot settle. His wife snores,
and wherever he goes in search of somewhere quieter
he is faced by further distractions. His son is still
playing with his toy aeroplanes, the clock in the living-
room ticks too loudly, the tap in the kitchen drips and
the various animal noises out in the garden are
intolerable. Just when he finally manages to nod off, it
is time to get up.

This picture book, first published in 1980, is still one
of the best of its kind. Told with a deliberate amount of
repetition, its chief glory is Jill Murphy's tellingly witty
illustrations. Not a trick is missed, from Mrs Bear's
incongruous hairnet to the arrival of a letter from the
Inland Revenue on the last page where the newly woken

Mr Bear is still struggling to come to his senses. Black-and-white sketches on one page are faced by glowing colours opposite, and each picture tells a story way beyond the words of the text, so that children can see Mr Bear taking his night-time snack even though there is no mention of this in the text itself. Illustrations are also full of the type of domestic clutter known in any family, from toys and books left on the floor to ghostly saucepans and cutlery seen piled up in the kitchen sink by night.

Pumpkin Soup

Helen Cooper (author/illustrator)

Corgi (pb)

Cat, Squirrel and Duck enjoy a close friendship,

2½ to 3½

2¹/₂ to 3¹/₂

symbolized by their joint preparation every day of some delicious pumpkin soup. Each has his or her own special role here until Duck decides that he'd like Squirrel's normal job of stirring the soup. A fight breaks out, with Duck eventually storming off in a temper. When he fails to return that night, the other two animals are bereft. Venturing out in an unsuccessful attempt to find him, they return home to discover that Duck has come back after all. He is now allowed to take on a new role when making the precious soup, but as the last picture makes clear there seem bound to be more quarrels in the near future.

Helen Cooper is a highly distinctive illustrator, filling her books with huge, atmospheric pictures which loom out at readers as if seen through a powerful magnifying glass. The woods where her characters live glow with autumnal colours, while the pumpkin patch itself swirls with huge leaves overshadowing groups of tiny insects. When Cat and Squirrel are imagining the type of accident their friend Duck may have suffered, the pictures show what they are thinking. The story accompanying these magical illustrations is quirky, informal and affectionate, showing small children both the rewards and the occasional strains that exist in all true friendships. A deserved winner of the Kate Greenaway Award for children's illustration in 1999, this delightfully different book has since proved highly popular. Look out for the same artist's *The Baby Who Wouldn't Go to Bed*, which won the same award in 1997.

The Runaway Bunny

Margaret Wise Brown (author) **Clement Hurd** (illustrator)
Collins (hb)

Little Bunny thinks it might be fun to run away. But when he puts this idea to his mother, the whole thing soon turns into an affectionate game. Whatever bizarre scheme Little Bunny suggests as a way of putting his plan into action, his resourceful parent promptly caps it with her own superior counter-strategies: if Little Rabbit decides to turn into a fish, she will become a fisherman, and if her son changes into a rock, then she will become a mountain climber. And so the good-humoured tussle goes on, until Little Rabbit finally runs out of ideas and declares "Shucks, I might as well stay where I am and be your little bunny." Clement Hurd's last picture shows the pair happily eating carrots

2½ to 3½

in a snug little burrow at the foot of an old tree. All the wilder fantasies in this story are illustrated too, with the mother at one point turning into a rabbit-shaped tree, for her son to fly home to when he decides to become a bird. Margaret Wise Brown had an extraordinary ability to reach the imagination of small children, and this classic story encapsulates the kind of absurd exchanges that can occur between parent and child. Small readers are likely to be reassured rather than oppressed by the notion of a mother's ubiquitous and all-pervading love.

The Runaway Train
Benedict Blathwayt (author/illustrator)
Red Fox (pb)

This picture book is also a work of art. On one dizzying two-page spread the artist provides a bird's eye view of miles of countryside, showing the intermingling of roads, railway lines and rivers while in the distance a small town is seen preparing for the night. Horses are led to the stables on a farm, while in the fields the last of the hay is being taken in – except for one particular stoop, behind which two young lovers lie basking in the setting sun. In the far corner, visitors to a ruined abbey stretch their legs, ready to return home. There are many other pages drawn with the same meticulous attention to detail, leaving infants with much to see and to

2¹/2 to 3¹/2

THE RUNAWAY TRAIN
Benedict Blathwayt

wonder at even after several readings. The story itself
has a regular refrain for everyone to join in as the
driver of the little red train repeatedly tries to catch up
with it after it unexpectedly departs without him. A
passing helicopter finally lends a hand while also
providing the illustrator with one more chance to show
his talents for picturing the world seen as if from high
in the air.

Sonny's Wonderful Wellies
Lisa Stubbs (author/illustrator)
Piccadilly Press (pb)

Ever since A.A. Milne wrote about a small child's "great
big waterproof boots" in a poem aptly named

2¹/₂ to 3¹/₂

"Happiness", Wellington boots have enjoyed a good press in children's books. Such popularity can only increase when they are also as brightly coloured as the red wellies worn by Sonny the duck in this engaging picture book. All he needs now is some rain to splash about in, but when none comes his granny fills up a paddling pool where he can frolic to his heart's content. What makes this little story even more effective is the amount of good-humoured detail contained on each page, from father duck going off to work with a newspaper under his wing, to the family's half-human, half-duck house. On the television there's a serial about duck spacemen; on the floor, a duck doll waits to be played with. Why a duck rather than a human infant? Animals have always acted as symbols for humans in literature, and in this book Sonny stands for all infants everywhere.

A Special Something

Jan Fearnley (author/illustrator)

Methuen (hb)

The little girl in this picture book knows that her pregnant mother has a special something in her tummy, but she's not sure exactly what. She imagines the different animals it might be – hippopotamus, dinosaur, crocodile, kangaroo, monkey – and all the various ways each one might prove a nuisance on arrival. Finally she discovers that the bump turns into a real-life baby brother, and is duly reconciled when her father takes a photograph of his two special somethings sitting happily together. This story deals with a small child's unease about a mother's pregnancy by picturing all her negative thoughts in terms of possible wild animals that might come into the house. The little girl in question can therefore remain "good" in her own and in her parents' eyes while expressing resentment in a way that offends nobody. In fact, all the animals she chooses are also her toys, seen on the cover taking a ride in her baby pram. Toys often serve as scapegoats upon whom children can take out occasional bursts of anger in a way that they can't within the family itself. This clever picture book contains no hint of preaching or condescension. With accompanying illustrations that are consistently witty as well as attractive, it comes over as great fun and also, in a more subtle way, very understanding.

2¹/₂ to 3¹/₂

We're Going on a Bear Hunt

Michael Rosen (author) **Helen Oxenbury** (illustrator)

Walker Books (hb & pb)

One reason so many small children make their way to
the parental bed on weekend mornings is the chance of
a really good imaginative game played either with each
other or, if they are lucky, with a parent. This charming
picture book is about exactly such a game, with dad
leading three small children on an imaginary bear hunt
involving crossing cold rivers, muddy fields and thick
forests before finally arriving at a dark cave. All these
imaginary encounters are reproduced in this picture
book by Helen Oxenbury as if they had actually
happened. Colour watercolours alternate with black-
and-white illustrations, both perfectly capturing that
mixture of delight and mild apprehension
characterizing the kind of game in which the child
never quite knows what's going to happen next. When
the bear is finally confronted there is a mad rush home,
finishing up with everyone hiding under the duvet on
the double bed where the whole story has been acted
out all the time. Michael Rosen, a brilliant children's
poet, here creates a minimal but highly imaginative
text, which includes some lively, made-up words for the
various sound effects. Dramatic and comic at the same
time, this prize-winning book is a constant delight.

2½ to 3½

Where Are You, Blue Kangaroo?

Emma Chichester Clark (author/illustrator)

Andersen Press (hb) HarperCollins (pb)

Lily is always leaving Blue Kangaroo behind
somewhere, even though she is quite devoted to him.
On a visit to the park he is left on top of a slide, and
later only the kindness of a lady in a pink hat saves him
from being abandoned in a London bus. Finally, after
an undignified escapade at the zoo where he ends up
pushed into a real kangaroo pouch, the stuffed toy has
had enough. Hiding in the pocket of Lily's dressing
gown, he gives her such a fright that she never lets him
out of her sight again. How exactly this happens is best
left to this delightful picture book to tell for itself. The
sequel to the same artist's *I Love You, Blue Kangaroo*, it's
illustrated with the cool wit and visual elegance always
such a feature with this artist. Pages filled with different
urban types alternate with scenes of sun and flowers.
Lily herself is always the dominant character,
demanding and vocal as well as affectionate and fun-
loving. Blue Kangaroo himself stays fairly impassive
throughout, which is perhaps just as well given the high
emotion he creates in the person who loves him most –
but who still cannot always remember not to leave him
behind.

2¹/₂ to 3¹/₂

Where the Wild Things Are

Maurice Sendak (author/illustrator)

Bodley Head (hb) Red Fox (pb)

One of the most celebrated picture books ever created, this story was initially thought too frightening for small children in Britain after it was published in America in 1963. Finally appearing over here in 1967, it has never ceased to delight parents and children alike. This is because although there are indeed some fearsome monsters in these pages, they are all instantly tamed by "the most wild thing of all", Max himself, the infant hero of this story. Beasts with terrible teeth, eyes and claws are shown turning into Max's humble followers, who then want nothing more than for him to stay with them for ever, playing wild games together in the middle of the jungle. Max decides otherwise, and leaves them declaring undying love for him as he makes for the home he had previously abandoned.

As with all imaginary monsters, those featured here

2½ to 3½

are shown as originating from Max's own fantasies. The model for them is of course himself, and at the very start readers see him dressed in his own wolf suit complete with bushy tail, leaping about and behaving so roughly that his mother herself calls him a "wild thing" and sends him off to be on his own as punishment. But Max imagines that he is somewhere else, transforming his bedroom into a jungle in the process (his bedposts gradually growing into trees while his carpet slowly turns into long grass). The actual images of the monsters he meets come from one of his own pictures, pinned to the wall at the bottom of the stairs. What finally brings him down to earth is the smell of the food that his mother leaves in his room. He has now got over his tantrum, symbolized here by six wordless pages showing Max and his fellow-monsters swinging from trees, dancing to the moon, jumping in the air and careering along in a grotesque procession.

After such a display of anger when young it's natural to feel remorse, which is why Max is now ready to hurry back "to be where someone loved him best of all". Sendak's illustrations throughout are unforgettable, while in only a few words his text describes a young child's temper and how it can be defused in a way that readers of any age will immediately understand. Despite many other fine works to his credit, Sendak has never created anything better than this wonderful picture book.

2¹/₂ to 3¹/₂

Where's My Teddy?
Jez Alborough (author/illustrator)
Walker Books (hb & pb)

This not-very-arresting title in fact disguises a dramatic and, for some, possibly a rather unsettling picture book. Eddy goes off to find his teddy, lost somewhere in a dark wood. Surrounded by tall trees Eddy looks increasingly small and even more so when he suddenly comes across a massive teddy ten times his size. But this is nothing compared to the next contrast in scale, when a truly giant mother bear comes stomping into the picture carrying Eddy's own teddy, now little more than a speck in her huge paws. Quickly switching teddies, both Eddy and the mother bear run away in different directions to the safety of their own beds.

Timid children may find the image of a small child lost in a forest a little frightening, not to mention the prospect of a brown bear so huge that she takes up an entire page. But what can frighten one child can always have the capacity to amuse another. For youngsters with strong nerves there is plenty to delight them here as they wait for the arrival of the huge bear following a deliciously scary walk through a forest that never looks safe for a moment. Eddy still appears somewhat scared once tucked up in bed, but then so too does the big bear, who throughout seems as frightened of Eddy as he is of her – quite a thought for young readers to

2½ to 3½

ponder. The same author-illustrator has also produced another book with the same cast, entitled *It's the Bear!*, in which the bear is not only huge but hungry as well. Infants with a taste for danger and who want

to hear more about Eddy's unwise picnic could well enjoy this story too.

2½ to 3½

151

2¹/₂ to 3¹/₂

Poetry

Books which tell a story in verse can always be extremely popular with children, particularly when a good tale is put across with strong rhymes and rhythms. Collections of individual poems may be initially less successful, since however brilliant, funny or atmospheric the poems may be, they rarely have the immediate attraction offered by a compelling story. Instead they tend to work more subtly in a child's imagination, offering them the opportunity of recalling odd lines or – if they prove really popular – learning the whole poem by heart.

Many fine poetry anthologies now exist, and the books that follow are particularly suitable for smaller children. Pictures are usually extensive, and there is an emphasis on action rather than imagination. Some of them suggest accompanying games, following on from a tradition where simple rhymes are associated with particular forms of play, either between adults and children or between children themselves. Children brought up on nursery rhymes should be used to lively verse that mixes everyday reality with wild imagination; the best of the poems selected below share some of this characteristic too.

As Quiet as a Mouse: A Rhyming Action Story

Hilda Offen (author/illustrator)

Red Fox (pb)

Each page of this charming book features a couple of lines of a poem along with instructions to the reader on the opposite page about what to do while they are listening. These suggestions range from "Put hand to ear" to "Pretend to sneeze" and "Snore". This all makes for great fun, with other suggestions including laughing, huffing-and-puffing, roaring and singing. These suggestions appear below a series of

2½ to 3½

153

pictures depicting an exuberant little boy performing the same actions himself. The poem itself is enjoyable enough, involving different animals all making a noise culminating in the visit of a dinosaur, after which there is a truly terrible din. But the little boy finally manages to put a stop to all this: "I made them be quiet, / It didn't take long. / Then they danced in a ring / And I sang them a song." The accompanying instruction here instructs readers to "Sing your favourite song", and such is the charm of this book that many young readers may want to follow all these various suggestions right up to this last one.

First Rhymes:
A Day of Rhymes, Games and Songs
Lucy Coats (author) **Selina Young** (illustrator)
Orchard Books (hb & pb)

These lively verses share some of the same subject-matter and energy found in nursery rhymes. Familiar characters put in an appearance, but in new contexts: "Humpty Dumpty stood on his head, / Humpty Dumpty fell out of bed. / All his silk carpets / And all his soft mats / Couldn't stop Humpty from going *Kersplat!*" Other rhymes describe adventures for new creations such as Young King Cole and My Grand Old Grandpa York. Divided into three sections, "Mornings",

2½ to 3½

"Afternoons" and "Evenings", the book's contents more or less follow the pattern of the normal day, starting with breakfast and ending with bedtime. There is plenty of noise along the way with all the various rhymes to clap, bounce, shout and dance to, illustrated to great effect by Selina Young. The longer poems can be read as short stories, with the tale of Jack and the Beanstalk a particularly good example of the poet's exuberant style: "The giant was snoring / Like ninety-nine trains, / Like forty-one diggers / Or ten creaky cranes." The traditionally violent ending appears in full here, but odd moments of aggression such as this are always presented as part of an atmosphere of riotous make-believe, and overall Lucy Coats achieves an effective mix of old and new in a book that is lively, unexpected and sometimes outrageous.

Hippety-Hop, Hippety-Hay: Growing with Rhymes from Birth to Age 3
Opal Dunn (author) **Sally Anne Lambert** (illustrator)
Frances Lincoln (hb & pb)

Opal Dunn is a language consultant, and she adds numbers of suggestions throughout this book on how best to use her collection of new and old rhymes. The book starts with traditional touching and singing games, and then goes on to rhymes involving hide-and-seek, pretend falls and knee-bouncing. Many parents will have been able to work out for themselves many of the accompanying games to these traditional poems, either through common sense or from their own experiences when young. But there is no harm in adding suggestions about possible play activities linked to various rhymes, especially when these are put across not as orders but simply as ideas worth trying out. The book caters for slightly older children, too, with some of the poems and games included here involving more sophisticated skills like counting, playing "I-Spy", and training in the merits of saying "Thank you!" The book ends with a new poem about road safety, exhibiting the same light touch and pleasant illustrations by Sally Anne Lambert that characterize the rest of its contents. Particularly suitable for nursery education, it also contains much for parents who are open to suggestions about how best to amuse and entertain their young children.

2½ to 3½

Husherbye
John Burningham (author/illustrator)
Jonathan Cape (hb) Red Fox (pb)

The first half of this book is about feeling tired; the last half describes actually being asleep. Written to rocking lullaby rhythms, each page tells a different story of pre-bedtime fatigue, and covers characters as diverse as a cat with a pram, a baby sailing a boat, three tired bears and a flying goose. First seen searching for rest, these characters are then revisited in the second part of the book where the cat has now managed to find a place, the baby is safely asleep, the three tired bears have crashed out in their beds and the goose is slumbering on a comfortable wicker chair. The artist includes drawings and colour paintings on each double-page spread, with the drawings sometimes describing what the characters have been doing beforehand (the three bears, for example, are exhausted because they've been

2½ to 3½

157

pushing a lorry loaded with luggage). While colour illustrations always appeal to children, drawings in black-and-white have their attraction too, particularly in this case where their soft lines enhance the dreamy atmosphere of the book. Young readers get the best of both worlds here, and from an artist who is always particularly good at depicting characters exuding their own sense of quiet dignity.

Out and About Through the Year

Shirley Hughes (author/illustrator)

Walker Books (hb & pb)

A small girl and her baby brother romp through the changing seasons in this book, finding something to enjoy in wind, rain and mist as well as in sunshine and snow. Starting with spring, the first poem announces its no-nonsense intentions loudly and clearly: "Shiny boots, / Brand new, / Pale shoots / Poking through, / In the garden, / Out and about, / Run down the path, / Scamper and shout. / Wild white washing / Waves at the sky, / The birds are busy / And so am I." Here the little girl and her dog are running down a garden path, with baby brother left hovering by the door. After that the pair splash in the mud, shop in the rain, and – when it gets warmer – play in the paddling pool. Then they go on a walk in the country, a day by the sea, a tiresome time in bed suffering a cold and finally snow and ice as Christmas arrives. Every now and again the artist presents a two-page spread without any words, showing how different families become involved in the various activities associated with each season. Backed up by simple and evocative rhymes, these illustrations are superb in their breadth of vision and depth of understanding.

2¹/₂ to 3¹/₂

Pre-school

$3^{1}/_{2}$ to 5

Pre-school

3¹/₂ to 5

Children between these ages should now be able to master more complex language, even though most of them will not as yet be anything like good readers themselves. But the stories they hear can afford to be more ambitious now in terms of sentence-length and the actual amount of words on any one page. Vocabulary itself can also be more developed, although as before children may still enjoy the sound of a particular word before they know its meaning. Beatrix Potter always believed in providing small children with what she called "fine-sounding words", and there are certainly plenty of those in her best tales (see p.219). Yet if the vocabulary of any story is too advanced for small readers, they will not on the whole get much out of it. A useful rule of thumb when choosing books for this age is to look at a typical page of text and count the number of words that might present some difficulty. If more than one in ten of the words seems too hard, the book is probably too difficult for the reader in mind.

Subject-matter in books at this level still often revolves around typical family situations, but young readers now often take an interest in other children of the same age. In response, a number of picture books concentrate on the topic of peer relations, often using animal characters but still getting over an essentially human message about how various individuals set about getting on with each other or not. Children may now be ready to discover more about the world further away from their own domestic scene and its immediate surroundings. Catering for this need are books that turn from the comfortably familiar to stories involving people, animals and scenery in very different countries. But however exotic the characters and their environment, how they think, feel and behave must still conform fairly closely to the way in which small readers continue to make sense of themselves and others. More complex studies of character must wait until an older age.

Illustrations can also afford to be more adventurous, hinting to the reader what is going on over and above anything stated directly in the text. Anthony Browne (see p.186) is a master of this particular skill, producing numbers of fine picture books that invariably reveal more each time they are read through. At a purely artistic level, pictures may also now contain more detail, with less risk of confusing young readers who might formerly have had some trouble sorting out what is important from what is simply decorative. But there are also popular illustrators for this age who present children with pictures that symbolize rather than simply reflect reality as they see it. In fact, the whole business of getting to know how an artist works, recognizing and enjoying their particular approach, and then anticipating what they might come up with next is just one of the many pleasures available to children from the brilliant, inventive and sometimes mind-boggling picture books recommended in this section.

3½ to 5

Stories

While stories for this age still tend to get most of their effects from humour, there is now often a more serious side to some of them. The almost universally happy endings still common for this age group may be joined by something approaching a moral lesson, particularly on the importance of good manners or, more generally, on being able to see things from a point of view other than one's own. Small children's natural egocentricity does not always lend itself very easily to such ability, which is perhaps one reason why stories for them often stress this particular aspect of growing-up.

It is often easiest at this age to absorb information which is presented in story form, given that children seem to have a natural feeling for fiction of all sorts. Turning everyday events into something of a story, whether this involves getting dressed, eating a meal or going for a walk, is something that parents have always done when it comes to finding the most effective way of getting small children to do what is required. Stories are also useful as easy ways of explaining something to a child, whether the particular explanation aims at being truthful or not. Fairy tales and legends, for example, are full of stories with fanciful – but, for small children, highly acceptable – explanations for various natural phenomena, such as why the sea is salty or why a mountain has a particular shape. When they get older, children will want more logical answers to such questions, but at this age they are happy with explanations that are often fantasy stories in themselves. That said, however, they also appreciate stories that try to get closer to the truth about things. The techniques of fiction have always been a good means of communicating child-friendly explanations of what actually happens in the outside world, simplified to a level where even small children have some hope of understanding the bare bones of quite complex issues.

Amazing Grace

Mary Hoffman (author) **Caroline Binch** (illustrator)
Frances Lincoln (hb & pb)

Grace always has a lively imagination, and when the chance to play Peter Pan comes up in a production at her primary school, she is keener than anyone else – even if other pupils object because she is both black and a girl. Her mother and grandmother tell her she can do anything if only she puts her mind to it, and Grace responds by winning the part and then doing both it and

Amazing Grace

Mary Hoffman · Caroline Binch

herself proud. Every child will appreciate Grace's quandary, especially those who have come to expect less of themselves than they should in a society of equals. Caroline Binch's illustrations jump from the page with energy and total conviction. At times Grace seems to gaze straight out at readers as if daring them not to accept everything that she does, from her various imaginary games where she acts all the parts herself to the moment when she finally triumphs on the school stage. A bestseller when it was first published in 1992, this story deserves to be in every school along with its equally impressive sequels, *Grace and Family* and *An Angel Like Me*.

Bad Habits!

Babette Cole (author/illustrator)

Puffin (pb)

Babette Cole is the "bad girl" of children's picture books, and teachers or parents of a delicate nature are strongly advised to go through all the pages first before buying any of her titles, just in case they come across something they find unacceptable. But for those with stronger constitutions, there is no doubt that she is also extremely funny, regularly breaking normal rules of decorum in pictures that burst from the page with a wicked energy all of their own. This book describes a

$3^1/2$ to 5

dreadful child called Lucretzia Crum, whose bad habits – graphically illustrated – include breaking wind, belching, spitting and swearing, all usually accompanied by her diabolical smile. When she finally goes too far, her father invents a series of preventive measures to contain her such as a "No Scream/Kick Tube" and a "Classroom Pacifier" (a steel cage within which she can be lowered outside the classroom allowing the teacher to get on with an orderly lesson). But despite everything Lucretzia remains wild – until, that is, her parents decide to invite some real monsters to her birthday party. These are so gross that Lucretzia and her equally appalling friends decide that it's time to behave better lest they too turn into such horrible beings.

There was a time in the history of children's literature when books were seen as important allies for parents in trying to instil good morals and acceptable manners into their children. Although this attitude helped produce some excellent books, it also led to numbers of pious and goody-goody ones, which – however popular with parents – often turned children off. Nowadays, books for young people are often more forthright in their approach, with the intention of getting closer to how real children are, both when they're being good and at those times when, unobserved by adults, forbidden language and actions erupt. Instead of hiding the worse side of children, such books encourage them to face up to their faults by admitting that they have them in the first place.

But although children's picture books by Babette Cole and others are more frank in describing the worst that children can do, this does not mean that bad behaviour is endorsed. This particular title, like all her other books, ends on a highly moralistic note, with Lucretzia now a "civilized little angel" with her very own halo floating above her head. By having fun with the whole idea of wicked behaviour, the hope is to make tyoung readers' own tantrums and occasional grossness seem too ridiculous to be worth bothering with next time. Parents (and children) happy with this way of doing things will find much to enjoy and laugh about. Others uneasy with such an approach are advised to steer well clear, both of this book and of other titles by the same outrageously funny writer-illustrator.

The Book about Moomin, Mymble and Little My

Tove Jansson (author/illustrator)
Sort of Books (hb)

Tove Jansson's Moomin books are usually directed at older children, but this particular picture book, full of eye-catching visual effects, has much to offer younger readers. It introduces some of the main characters in

3½ to 5

3½ to 5

the author's particular dream world, starting off with Moomintroll himself. Pictured as a half-hippopotamus, half-human, he is seen walking through some dark woods with a pail of milk. Holes cut into each page give clues of the story still to come. Moomin eventually meets Mymble, a more recognisably human being seen weeping over the loss of her sister. Various adventures follow, including an encounter with Gaffsie, a bad-tempered witch, and an unwanted journey into a vacuum cleaner wielded by the Hemulen, another of the author's peculiar but curiously reassuring creations. Everything ends happily with a final return to mother and a feast of pink berry juice. Before that, pictures glow with dark and light colours on pages that are frequently cut into odd shapes and sizes. This is really is a book like no other, offering readers a trip into the unpredictable but constantly appealing imagination of one of the truly great children's authors of the last fifty years. Translated over the years from the original Finnish into

35 different language, this new English version has been put into wittily rhyming verse by Sophie Hannah.

Can't You Sleep, Little Bear?

Martin Waddell (author) **Barbara Firth** (illustrator)
Walker Books (hb & pb)

The answer is no: Little Bear is feeling far too lively, but he is scared of the dark as well. To combat this fear, Big Bear – who could be either his father or grandfather – supplies him with larger and larger bedside lights, but even when the cave they live in is totally lit up Little Bear points out that it is still dark outside. So finally Big Bear takes him out of bed and carries him through the cave door. He then shows him how the moon and the stars have driven back the darkness from the forest.

There is an ingenious story-within-a-story here, since while all these negotiations are going on Big Bear is also trying to read a picture book himself. On closer inspection, this turns out to be a miniature version of the very same book as this one. Infants can puzzle out this paradox for themselves and they may also enjoy the way that each larger lantern supplied by Big Bear lights up more of the cave, eventually revealing toys, pictures and a cricket bat only dimly visible before. Parents who are trying to encourage their children not to keep the light on at night can use this book to show how benign

3½ to 5

the darkness appears here – and with it the strong suspicion that Little Bear is using his fear as little more than an excuse for staying up late. The images of soft cuddly love between the adult and child figures that run through this book, excellently illustrated by Barbara Firth, are also reassuring both for Little Bear and his readers. With such quantities of patient affection on tap, any lingering fear of the dark finally seems irrelevant when there is so much else also going on for Little Bear – and by implication every other loved infant – on each page of this captivating book.

Clown
Quentin Blake (illustrator)
Red Fox (pb)

Clowns have always combined pathos with humour, and both these qualities are on display in this stunning, text-less picture book. It begins with the clown and his other toy friends being dumped in a dustbin. He decides to escape, and spends the rest of the book trying to get help for those he has left behind. Repeatedly discarded by everyone he meets, he finally makes friends with a young girl who has been left by her mother to mind a lively toddler. They rescue the toys, and just make it back to the flat before the mother arrives. She in turn is delighted that everything is so

3½ to 5

tidy – entirely due to the clown, who also turns out to be a gifted cleaner and babyminder. All ends happily, with the clown and his friends now installed once again in a home where they are really appreciated.

The clown is befriended by small children throughout this story, and child readers in turn will almost certainly feel the same way about him too. Like them, he is small, comparatively powerless and at the mercy of an adult world that is not always very understanding. Readers know what he is thinking because of the pictures that occasionally appear in bubbles above his head, but the surrounding adult characters in the book just can't be bothered with his feelings at all. The clown therefore has to fight his own battles, first taming a savage dog by performing various tricks in front of him and later achieving the same effect with a bawling baby and his tearful junior helper. In the background the heavy traffic and varied skyline of London occasionally

3½ to 5

looms, reminding readers quite how small the clown is by comparison. Other subtle visual points abound, from the all-too-evident fatigue of the mother as she climbs up the stairs to her shabby high-rise flat to the complicit look shared between the clown and the girl when everything turns out so well at the end. With so much visual detail to look out for, this is a book that can always be returned to for its skill, humour and underlying humanity.

Cowboy Baby
Sue Heap (author/illustrator)
Walker Books (hb & pb)

Infants do not always want to go to bed, and Sue Heap's affectionate picture book explores this well-known situation in the form of a story played out by Cowboy Baby himself. His particular technique for spinning out the evening is to tell his Sheriff Pa that he has first to find Texas Ted, Denver Dog and Hank the Horse. But when these toys have been safely rounded up, Cowboy Baby and his gang then decide to hide in the desert. After Pa brings him down a star with a lasso, Cowboy Baby – now sworn in as an official deputy – is at last happy to go to bed and sleep. Sue Heap tells this story in rhythmical language close to poetry, and her illustrations are bright and bold, conjuring up the sort of cowboy desert landscape of every child's imagination. Sheriff Pa is a perpetually smiling figure with all the time in the world to chase after his playful son.

Crispin: The Pig Who Had it All
Ted Dewan (author/illustrator)
Doubleday (hb) Corgi (pb)

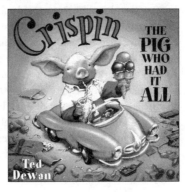

Crispin is a little pig with rich parents but no one to play with. All his expensive presents soon end up broken, whether these are robot Teddy Bears or Giga-Pigstations offering every latest computer game. One Christmas he receives a huge wrapped box, but when he opens it there is nothing inside. Crispin throws it away, but when other humanized animals come to play in it, he eventually makes new friends and realizes that imaginary games with others are always the best.

Ted Dewan is one of an interesting and innovative

3¹/₂ to 5

younger generation of author-illustrators whose pictures mix dreamlike imagery with meticulous detail. The house where Crispin lives is a futuristic building with lavishly curved staircases and a strong sense of ostentatious wealth. His parents, depicted mooching around in designer bathrobes or sitting in state-of-the-art armchairs, are no help at all in their son's search for something to do. When he finally discovers the world of imaginary play with friends, the illustrations practically burst with colour, movement and a feeling of energy that has at last found some proper release. Pictured at first in an expensive model car, clutching an ice-cream in one hand and a fizzy drink in the other, it is hard for readers to accept that Crispin is actually a deprived little pig. But by the end of his story there is no doubt that he is now much better off than before in ways that money can never buy. For such insights plus all its visual inventiveness, this is an excellent book for readers just beginning to think for themselves.

Dr. Dog
Babette Cole (author/illustrator)
Red Fox (pb)

This picture book is not just good rude fun but also educative, though always in a rather naughty way. Its hero, Dr. Dog, is a canine consultant to an unhealthy

family called the Gumboyles. He gives its various members sound advice about the dangers of smoking, catching nits from using other people's combs and contracting worms through not washing hands after visits to the toilet. But when it comes to failing to convince Grandad about the inadvisability of eating too many baked beans combined with large quantities of beer, playground humour takes over as the obstinate old man's windy eruptions finally blow the roof right off the house. Children are likely to find this the funniest moment in any picture book that they have ever seen, and so too may many adults. For those who dislike such earthy humour – you have at least been warned! But Babette Cole's sense of humour extends well beyond lavatory jokes: every picture in this book radiates such a strong sense of mischievous fun it is almost impossible not to grin back in return.

Dogger
Shirley Hughes (author/illustrator)
Bodley Head (hb) Red Fox (pb)

Dogger is a stuffed toy dog greatly loved by his young owner Dave, so when he goes missing there are long faces all round until he turns up. All children will feel for Dave here – even those who've never made a particular toy or whatever into the type of "transitional object" that psychologists believe gives small children a sense of security at an early stage of development. Parents will also enjoy this book, since Shirley Hughes has built up a reputation as an illustrator who is able to capture the authentic flavour of contemporary life. Her tousled children, untidy houses, busy streets and homely young mums and dads can seem closer to reality than reality itself, and her understanding of children – their mood swings, enthusiasms and occasional unhappinesses – is unparalleled. This title is one of her most popular, but any book of hers has that special way of getting things absolutely right.

Don't Step on the Crack!
Colin McNaughton (author/illustrator)
HarperCollins (hb & pb)

Trying not to step on the cracks between paving stones

is just one of a number of the minor neuroses that some children – and adults, for that matter – adopt from time to time as a way of controlling the various

anxieties in their lives. In this exuberant picture book, Colin McNaughton seeks to make such mini-obsessions seem ridiculous by sending them up in a way that makes it almost impossible ever to take them seriously again. Here, treading on a crack is shown to be an act as likely to turn you into a pig as it is to transform you into someone of the opposite sex. Even worse, it might encourage Dad to regain his lost youth

by becoming a hippie or Mum to go in for a disastrous new look, involving lots of bare midriff balanced above massively high platform shoes. By this time even a truly nervous toddler might well be laughing, especially at

3½ to 5

another picture showing a little boy setting off to school without his trousers – yet another occasion where the cracks in the pavement have worked their evil magic. Children with similar worries might now feel encouraged to laugh at them too. If such feelings run too deep for that, readers still have the satisfaction of contemplating anxieties so ludicrously exaggerated that any of their own will seem fairly modest by comparison.

Colin McNaughton is of course not the first writer to approach this topic: A.A. Milne wrote about it years ago in the poem "Lines and Squares", found in his anthology *When We Were Very Young* (see p.242). There he depicted Christopher Robin dreading the masses of bears waiting for anyone who trod on a crack in the pavement, though Ernest Shepard's drawings defused any tension by depicting the bears as more like amiable pussycats. Colin McNaughton's book is a worthy successor.

The Enormous Crocodile
Roald Dahl (author) **Quentin Blake** (illustrator)
Puffin (pb)

An enormous crocodile boasts that he is going to eat a child for lunch, and to that wicked end scuttles off to the nearest town. But however ingenious his various disguises – he pretends to be a palm tree, then a seesaw and finally a park bench – the children always know when to run away from him. This is because the crocodile is constantly unmasked by the various other animals in the jungle that he has attacked or insulted on his previous journey. Finally the elephant throws the crocodile up to the sun where "he was sizzled up like a sausage!"

Roald Dahl was famous for his love of mock-violence, and there is plenty of detail here about the particular taste and texture of small children as imagined by the greedy crocodile. But the sheer exaggeration of this story also communicates the fact that all these events happen safely in the land of the absurd. If there is still any lingering doubt on this score, Quentin Blake's illustrations are so funny that even the crocodile himself comes over as more a pantomime monster than anything like the real thing, This is quite a long text for small children, but Dahl was always a skilful storyteller and young readers are likely to stay interested until the very end.

Frog and the Stranger
Max Velthuijs (author/illustrator)
Milet Ltd (hb) Andersen Press (pb)

A rat moves into a settled and distinctly smug riverside

3½ to 5

community consisting of a duck, a pig and a frog. But while the other animals mutter about "dirty rats", Frog decides to make friends with the new arrival, who may look a bit scruffy but otherwise seems industrious and law-abiding.

He soon discovers that the rat, who has travelled all over the world and can speak three languages, is in fact both interesting and obliging. The rest of the animal community

Max Velthuijs
Frog and the Stranger

remains hostile until the rat intervenes in a series of accidents, each time helping others with no thought for himself.

The overall message of tolerance for others different from ourselves is so clear in this book that even the youngest reader will realize what the score is. Such books are unlikely to change intolerant behaviour in real life on their own unless actively backed up by example at home, but they can still be useful as a way of

3½ to 5

opening up discussion with the young about important issues such as irrational prejudice against others. Dedicated "to all animals on this earth, whatever their colours or shade", this book is also illustrated with wit and an eye for the ludicrous. Its slightly mournful-looking caricatures make a nice change from the constantly grinning animals found in other picture books, and the details of the rat's untidy camp (a bottle leaning against the tent, other objects scattered about) reflect the natural untidiness of small children themselves. Max Velthuijs, a Dutch artist who writes in English, has produced many picture books for children. Each one possesses a distinctive style that combines simplicity with a good eye for the subtle quirks of character that distinguish one being from another.

3½ to 5

Further Frog Books

Frog is Frog
Frog is a Hero
Frog in Love
Frog and Pig
Frog in Winter
Frog and Hare

Frog Finds a Friend
Frog is Frightened
Frog and a Very
    Special Day
Frog and the Birdsong
Frog and the
    Wide World

Gorilla

Anthony Browne (author/illustrator)

Walker Books (hb & pb)

3½ to 5

One of the finest works of its generation, this picture book offers readers a feast of visual clues in the course of narrating a comparatively simple story. Hannah, who lives alone with her rather remote father, is obsessed by gorillas even though she has never seen one. One night, she dreams that the toy gorilla her father has given her as a birthday present has turned into a real one. Together they steal from the house out into the dark, swinging through the trees to the local zoo. A visit to the cinema followed by a meal out finally ends with a trip back home, with Hannah and her gorilla dancing together on the lawn before saying goodnight.

Like Hannah herself, Anthony Browne is also obsessed by gorillas. The book's cover shows the large gorilla who becomes Hannah's special friend while in the background King Kong appears in silhouette on top of a chimney and another gorilla is seen dancing in a window. On the opening page, there is a photograph of a gorilla in the father's newspaper, a picture of another on Hannah's cereal packet and the shadow of a third on the kitchen floor. And so it goes on, with a reproduction of the *Mona Lisa* and the Statue of Liberty both sporting gorilla faces while yet another gorilla is seen looming out of a garden hedge. But all this is much more than a simple matter of finding the hidden object. The gorilla in this story gives Hannah the attention and kindness she misses from her father. But by the final page, when the father at last shows some affection and offers her a trip to the zoo, he is made to look in silhouette just like the gorilla the little girl had previously invented as a parent substitute. Colour also plays a crucial role here. At the start of the story the chilly greens and white of the kitchen emphasize the coldness of the father, but by the end he is wearing bright clothes in a room itself glowing with warm colours. No detail in any picture book by Anthony Browne gets there by accident; there is always an overall artistic plan whereby emotional situations implicit in the story are reinforced by everything that appears in the illustrations. This is a book that children can pore over for hours and still find something new to think about. It is also a humane and compassionate study of loneliness, compensation and the recovery of a strong parental love that had temporarily forgotten how to show itself.

3½ to 5

The Gruffalo
Julia Donaldson (author) **Alex Scheffler** (illustrator)
Macmillan (hb & pb)

Told in verse, this story follows an old tradition where the small and the weak are shown eventually getting the better of the strong and powerful. Always an especially popular theme with children for obvious enough reasons, it features a tiny mouse who sees off attempts on his life from a fox, an owl, a snake and finally a hungry gruffalo. A what? Well, the gruffalo shown here is a type of monster invented by the mouse to frighten away other animals but who then, somewhat disconcertingly, comes to life himself. But in the end the mouse is up to scaring him away as well, ending the story alone and peacefully eating a nut. Small children soon learn that in nature some animals do indeed kill and eat others. Yet while they enjoy the type of suspense possible in those stories where this seems about to happen, unsurprisingly they do not want to see sympathetic small animals gobbled up by much larger ones.

3½ to 5

188

This charming story wins on all counts: flirting with the idea of danger in a way that makes it exciting to read and think about, but substituting a happy ending when something more realistic could come across as too upsetting. Alex Scheffler's forest pictures show a well-ordered green universe, ideal for all its wild inhabitants if only the occasional predator would leave them alone. Children with sometimes obstreperous older siblings may find this message particularly to their taste, which may be one reason why this good-humoured picture book has been so successful with small readers.

3½ to 5

Harold and the Purple Crayon
Crockett Johnson (author/illustrator)
Bloomsbury (hb) HarperCollins (pb)

This small picture book shows how Harold, hardly more than a baby himself, draws his way to adventure by using his ever-present purple crayon. He first sketches a road he can walk up and then draws an apple tree to stop by, and, since the apples are not yet ripe, Harold quickly produces a dragon to guard them. This proves so frightening that Harold finds he has unintentionally created a wavy sea because his purple crayon was shaking so much. And so it goes on, until Harold finally draws his bedroom window so that he can climb in through it and go to sleep. The purple crayon's single broad line as it sketches a series of basic, two-dimensional objects makes this an exceptionally easy picture book to follow. There is also something very satisfying for infants in the idea of a small child being able to create his own realities in this way. Parents and teachers might be tempted to provide children always with the brightest and fullest picture books they can find. But cutting down on detail and communicating through simple but memorable forms also has a place in the picture book world, and never more so than in the case of this little book, first published in 1955 and still going strong today.

Jamela's Dress

Niki Daly (author/illustrator)

Frances Lincoln (hb & pb)

Niki Daly is a brilliant South African illustrator, and this story, set in modern Cape Town, glows with bright colours from first to last. Jamela's mother buys some beautiful material for a wedding, but her daughter ruins it after proudly processing down the street

3½ to 5

wearing her mother's high-heeled shoes and with the precious cloth draped over her shoulders. But all is put right in the end, with enough of the material left over for a smart wedding dress for Jamela as well.

The book starts with a picture of Nelson Mandela on the wall of a shop, but it soon moves away from politics in favour of ordinary people. Jamela marches past a car mechanic, a photographer and a lady carrying chickens, always followed by a good-humoured band of other children. Dogs and bikes zoom by, with everyone laughing both at and with the little girl. When she is scolded by her mother she looks properly contrite, but a reconciliation isn't far away, and when it arrives it's accompanied by hugs and games. Few British children will have had the chance of visiting South Africa, but picture books as brilliant as this one convey a powerful impression of what it is like to be somewhere so different. Its message – that humans everywhere are the same in many ways but very different in some – is always worth attending to, especially when readers are still at a highly impressionable age. In the past small children often turned to books to get some idea of those people or places they knew nothing about. TV now gives them plenty of information about many things, but when it covers life abroad it is often in the context of some political or economic crisis thought to be newsworthy. Picture books such as this one focus instead on the type of domestic detail from everyday

3¹/₂ to 5

life in foreign countries too often omitted on the screen
– however meaningful to a young audience. This title is
just one among many illustrated books now available
that set out to widen British children's horizons in a
way that is entertaining at the same time.

Katie Morag Delivers the Mail

Mairi Hedderwick (author/illustrator)

Red Fox (pb)

3½ to 5

Katie lives in the village shop and post office on the
remote Isle of Struay in Scotland. An illustrated map on
the front pages shows where everyone else lives too,
with the mainland glimpsed looming in the distance.
Mail and supplies arrive every Wednesday, and because
baby brother Liam is cutting his first tooth and needs
constant attention, Katie is given the job of delivering
five parcels. An accidental fall into a pond means that
four of the addresses get washed away, but with
Granny's help everything gets sorted out in the end.

Mairi Hedderwick lived on a Hebridean island herself
for nine years, and this portrait of the fictional Struay
reflects her own knowledge of such a place and its way
of life. Transport is by bike, boat or tractor, and
Wellington boots are a sensible form of footwear for
most of the time. Katie's Granny is a tough sheep
farmer, surrounded by dogs, cats and chickens in a

kitchen full of clutter. When she and Katie drive home everyone waves at them, and small readers too will soon get the feeling that they also know everyone and everything about this little island, the subject of numbers of other titles featuring the same little girl. It has been said that Katie Morag leads the life that country dreams are made of, and the vision here of a close-knit and affectionate rural community is certainly very enticing. The artist always draws with a light touch, using watercolours to capture the soft hues of the island's fields and streams set against the darker shapes of the mountain ranges in the background.

3¹/2 to 5

Little Beaver and the Echo

Amy MacDonald (author) **Sarah Fox-Davies** (illustrator)

Walker Books (hb & pb)

Little Beaver lives on his own surrounded by a range of mountains. He is lonely, mistaking his own echo on the other side of a lake for a possible companion. Setting out in a canoe to trace the echo, he picks up a duck, an otter and a turtle on the way, so making the friends he was looking for all the time. This pleasing if simple story is made truly memorable by the quality of its illustrations. Children brought up in towns or suburbs will wonder at the vistas of huge, open countryside revealed within these pages. Although its animal characters talk like humans, they look exactly like the wildlife they represent down to the last detail. Huge water lilies, towering fir trees, a beaver's makeshift house and a lake shimmering with reflections also establish an atmosphere that is magical but utterly convincing. Picture books for children often present the natural world and its various inhabitants in terms of knockabout humour, but this book captures some of the awe-inspiring scenery found in the wild in a way unlikely to be forgotten by any of its readers.

Little Hotchpotch

Brian Patten (author) **Michael Terry** (illustrator)
Bloomsbury (hb & pb)

A shy little creature looks at its reflection in a pond, but can see only its own eyes, as big and bright as the moon. It asks a passing polar bear, "Excuse me please, can you tell me who I am?" But the bear cannot answer this question, and nor can any of the other animals it consults. Each recognizes one feature, but no one can come up with a final answer. Finally the wise old owl puts everyone right: it's the rarest, most wonderful creature of all – a Little Hotchpotch! Brian Patten brings a poet's touch to the text with descriptions such as "wings that glitter like cathedral windows", but the real glory of this skilful accumulative story is found in

Michael Terry's extraordinary illustrations. Each picture
shows a detail of the little creature, which is then
represented in full on the next creature it consults. Its
exotically coloured feathers therefore anticipate the
parrot on the following page, just as its long, black
snout looks forward to the anteater on the next. Using a
combination of bright colour and meticulous detail, the
artist invests all the animals that follow the little
creature around in this simple but satisfyingly repetitive
text with a quality of belief that makes them seem real
and alive. Whether young readers will be satisfied by
the final revelation that the main hero is a creature that

has never existed is another matter, but most parents should not mind a little extra explaining for a picture book as luminous and captivating as this.

Little Pig Figwort
Henrietta Branford (author) **Claudio Muñoz** (illustrator)
HarperCollins (hb & pb)

3¹/₂ to 5

Little Pig Figwort simply can't get to sleep on the double bed where his other brothers and sisters are happily "sweet-dreaming the night away". So he decides to go on some adventures instead, starting with deep-sea diving in his own miniature submarine before going on a trip to the North Pole and finally ending with a journey to the moon. After that he's more than ready for his sleep back home, where finally "he cuddled and muddled down into the heap" made up of his less restless siblings. Henrietta Branford was a writer of great distinction, and this story shows all her usual care and inventiveness with words and phrases designed to reverberate in children's memories long after the story is finished. She is joined by the illustrator Claudio Muñoz, experienced as a cartoonist as well as an artist. His depictions of all the various different positions adapted by Figwort in his search for slumber combine the artist's own brand of visual shorthand with a strong sense of fun. Without realizing it, children going through more ambitious picture books such as this will also be learning something about the techniques of modern art as well, put across here in a way that is always strongly user-friendly.

3½ to 5

Mister Magnolia
Quentin Blake (author/illustrator)
Jonathan Cape (hb)

Britain has a long tradition of producing ingenious nonsense rhymes and stories for children, and in this book Quentin Blake shows he is well up with the other masters of this particular art. There is no logic in what Mister Magnolia does, nor any reason why he should be dressed in a striped waistcoat, blue jacket, yellow trousers and an outsized bow tie. The fact that he also has only one boot, the regular refrain running through the entire book, comes as little surprise. Easy rhyming verse tells readers how he plays the trumpet, gives rides to his friends on his scooter, juggles with fruit and has a pet dinosaur. The story ends with handstands and dancing to celebrate the arrival at last of another boot, even though this in no way matches what Mister

Magnolia is already wearing on his other foot.

The chief delight of this book lies in its uniquely child-friendly style of illustration. Having started his career as a cartoonist, Quentin Blake has always preferred to work with

rapid, sketchy pen-and-ink lines, which are then sometimes washed over in watercolour. Full of movement and energy, his pictures stop at just the moment when everything they want to suggest is there within them. If there is enough of an owl, a mouse, a frog or whatever else showing on the page, then it's time to go on to something else. The overall effect is of one long and riotous party packed with beaming characters joining in for all they are worth. The scribbled objects that abound in his pictures are easy for infants to pick out since they are usually set against

plain white or coloured backgrounds. With everyone
having such a good time in these pictures, young
readers in their thousands have found themselves
joining in the fun as well. But anyone thinking that
Blake's distinctively spontaneous style is easy to imitate
will soon discover – if they try – that the speed with
which he draws disguises years of practice allied to an
unrivalled eye for comic detail.

3½ to 5

The Mousehole Cat
Antonia Barber (author) **Nicola Bayley** (illustrator)
Walker Books (hb & pb)

Based on an old Cornish legend, this beautiful picture
book features old Tom and his cat Mowzer. Their life
together in the little fishing village of Mousehole is
tranquil enough until one day appalling weather
arrives, personified here as a visit from the Great Storm
Cat. Trapped in the village by huge waves that seem as
if they will never go away, everyone is threatened with
starvation until old Tom, accompanied by his faithful
cat, decides to go it alone in a quest for fish. Out in the
ocean, Mowzer discovers a way of taming the Great
Storm Cat, and her master eventually returns to the
village with enough fish for all.

This is quite a long story for younger children, but
easy enough to follow because of its simple structure.

Its loving references to food, available in the village in abundance to begin with and later notable by its absence, will not be lost on children with a healthy interest in what goes into their own stomachs. More difficult to understand is the whole concept of the Great Storm Cat as a symbol of the storm itself, but this problem is solved by Nicola Bayley's superb illustrations. Painted with the finest of brushes, the storm at sea looks both real and cat-like, with a mini-whirlwind turning into a giant paw and massive waves settling into the contours of a feline body. Elsewhere, individual pictures of the village glow like jewels, with cottages, fishing nets, cobbled streets and lobster pots all picked out in minute detail. The final picture, showing Mousehole lit up with a lamp at every window, is also a

3½ to 5

reference to the fish-feast held in the actual Cornish village of that name every year on the night before Christmas Eve. The artist adds numbers of friezes and illustrated borders throughout the book so that readers pass from scenes of sky and underwater life on one page to strips showing sea and the stars on the next. The deserved winner of a British Book Award for the best illustrated children's book of its year, this unforgettable work should give hours of pleasure to readers fascinated by its wealth of detail and its engaging narrative.

Not Now, Bernard

David McKee (author/illustrator)

Red Fox (pb)

Bernard just cannot get either of his preoccupied parents to take an interest in him. Even when he is shown eaten and then replaced by a monster the same indifference still holds sway. Although this monster then behaves quite badly, playing with his food and breaking a toy, he still goes meekly to bed when the time comes, unable to persuade the mother that he must now be taken more seriously. Young readers will quickly realise that the monster in question remains Bernard all the time, with his new appearance merely reflecting the increasingly resentful way that he's

3½ to 5

feeling. While they will all sympathize with him, whether in human or monster shape, parents reading this picture book will also be reminded of what it is like

to be pestered by a child when all they want to do is get on with something else. With the minimum of text and a series of pictures that reveal more each time they are looked at, David McKee has created a book of immediate psychological understanding which is also fun to read. First published in 1980, it has already turned into a nursery classic. Sharp-eyed readers will notice a model of Elmer the elephant sitting in Bernard's bookshelf, another popular character produced by this clever and insightful author-illustrator.

3½ to 5

The Owl Who Was Afraid of the Dark

Jill Tomlinson (author) **Paul Howard** (illustrator)

Mammoth (hb & pb)

Children who are themselves still somewhat frightened of the dark will easily understand why Plop, a baby owl, has similar feelings. His parents wisely decide to solve the problem by sending him to interview a variety of humans and animals who adore the darkness, with each one giving Plop their own special reasons for doing so. Finally Plop is converted, and flies off with his parents next night for some companionable hunting. This story, first published in 1968, provides some ingenious variations on the theme of darkness being good rather than bad. Paul Howard's memorable illustrations, added to this new edition which appeared in 2000, make the book even more remarkable. His night scenes capture all the peace and mystery of a landscape under moonlight. Villages huddle in the distance, stars gleam in the sky and trees turn into a darker shade of green. Just as beautiful are the illustrations of the family of owls, sitting on a branch to watch a firework display, its sudden explosions reflected in their huge eyes. The firework display itself is put forward as one reason for preferring the darkness – since otherwise it would not have shown up so well. Nervous toddlers, still unconvinced by these arguments, may not be able to explain exactly why they still can't get used to the dark.

3¹/₂ to 5

3½ to 5

But this book does at least open up what can be quite a delicate topic between parents and children, and one that is always better out in the open rather than being left in the dark itself.

Q Pootle 5
Nick Butterworth (author/illustrator)
HarperCollins (hb & pb)

On its way to a moon party, a spaceship makes a crash landing on Earth, shedding springs, bolts, and the odd apple core in the process. Fortunately for its driver, an amiable alien called Q Pootle 5, a frog, three birds and a cat called Colin lend a hand and help him fix the broken rocket booster, all so that he can make the party in time. This story offers small children an extremely child-friendly introduction to the wonders of space travel, starting off with three pages of sound effects skilfully caught in comic-strip type pictures and finishing with the moon party itself, illustrated by a four-page pullout display where other space people are depicted enjoying a meal of Saturn Rings, Star Biscuits and UFO Cake. Nick Butterworth is a talented and inventive illustrator, and his *Percy the Park Keeper* series

QPootle 5

NICK BUTTERWORTH

3½ to 5

has been a phenomenal hit with younger readers. Although this picture book is quite different, its final picture of Earth in the distance surrounded by stars manages to create an awesome effect which contrasts wonderfully with all the fun going on at the party below.

The Rascally Cake

Jeanne Willis (author) **Korky Paul** (illustrator)

Puffin Books (pb)

3½ to 5

Here is another picture book that some adults may not take to immediately but which many children will find very attractive indeed. It stars one Rufus Skumskins O'Parsely, whose eating preferences are truly disgusting. Brown rat roast, snotty handkerchiefs, fingernail clippings and even a jug of spit are among his favourite ingredients. Finally he makes a cake so revolting that the horrible mixture turns into a man-eating monster in its own right. But the one bite the monster takes of Rufus proves so nasty that it disappears without trace, leaving its victim a reformed character who now eats only the plainest food available.

Even the nicest-seeming children sometimes show a taste for yucky detail, of the type that should certainly never be discussed at table. Such pleasantries – also found in some of the oldest playground rhymes – are usually kept for the ears of other children at moments when adults are not around. Jokes of this type satisfy the part of children that still longs to remain gross and uncivilized – however well-behaved they may be for the rest of the time. A lot of the taboos once held sacrosanct in children's literature are now regularly broken and many children with a well-developed sense of coarseness may well fall on this book in delighted disbelief. The illustrator Korky Paul has an eye for maggots, mould and other such grossness, while Jeanne Willis tells her sorry tale in rhyming verses that are always easy on the ear. Children of a quieter disposition might not enjoy it to the same degree – but they also might surprise their parents by liking it very much. Discovering that others secretly think the same things can always be reassuring when young. Discovering them reproduced in a book written and illustrated by two adults can sometimes be even better.

3½ to 5

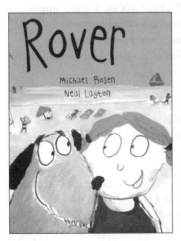

Rover
Michael Rosen
(author) **Neil Layton**
(illustrator)
Bloomsbury
(hb & pb)

Rover is the name given to the little girl of the house by the pet dog who lives there as well and who also tells this story. He understands quite a lot about humans, although always strictly from a canine point of view. He finds the "loud, coloured box" that Rover likes watching very boring, and cannot understand on a trip to the beach why so many people lie down and pretend to be dead after ripping off their clothes. But when Rover goes wandering off and gets lost it's the dog who manages to find her, and the happily reunited family finally returns home in another "family box" feeling greatly relieved. Michael Rosen's caustic wit makes the most of the humour that arises from seeing humans from a dog's viewpoint. The illustrations by Neal Layton continue this comic vein, combining scribbly pencil drawings with the brightest of colour washes. The dazzling display that results perfectly complements a combination of comedy and adventure, which is entertaining while also offering food for thought at the same time.

The Sandcastle

M.P. Robertson (author/illustrator)
Frances Lincoln (hb)

Having built his best-ever sandcastle on the beach, Jack wishes that it could somehow turn into the real thing – with himself as king. Waking up that night, he finds his dream has come true. Walking through the drawbridge, he is met by a fanfare of trumpets and is led through a cheering crowd to a throne made of seashells. But just as it always does on the beach, the sea eventually comes crashing in, with Jack highly relieved when his wish to return home to bed is granted at the last minute. This rather slight story is made memorable by the grandeur of its illustrations. The actual castle Jack builds for himself is memorable enough, but the real one he moves into at night is practically heart-stopping in its magnificence. Minstrels play and jesters joke as Jack, still dressed in pyjamas and a dressing gown, dances with the blue-eyed little girl he meets at the gatehouse. Any child who has made sandcastles and tried to defend them against the incoming tide will have had fantasies like this one, but few will have conjured up images quite as wonderful as those on these pages. The best picture books often take popular daydreams and return them to the child greatly embellished with an author-artist's own imaginative additions – and this one is a particularly good case-in-point.

Slinky Malinki
Lynley Dodd (author/illustrator)
Ragged Bears (hb) Puffin (pb)

Told in easy rhyming verse, this is the story of a cat who is cheerful and friendly during the day but at night turns into a dedicated thief. Finally discovered and disgraced, he decides to reform and the next time "whispers of wickedness stirred in his head, he adjusted his whiskers and stayed home instead". Infants often wonder what else really goes on when they are fast asleep in bed, and this likeable story gives them one answer. Set mostly at night under a full moon, we see Slinky Malinki peering round gates, padding along fences and stealing through doors. The objects he takes home become increasingly unlikely – a clock and some bottles, a pair of blue jeans – but readers won't mind once they get the idea that here is a cat who steals just for the sake of it. There is an ancient tradition in literature of celebrating romantic law-breakers like pirates or highwayman before finally seeing to it that they are punished (or at least reformed) by the final page, and Slinky Malinki is one such villain, offering his readers all the excitement of seeing someone doing something forbidden and then the final satisfaction of witnessing the same person humbled by the end of the story. Lynley Dodd's illustrations are consistently witty and atmospheric, and for readers who want to hear more about her dubious hero, *Slinky Malinki's Catflaps* provides an equally engaging sequel.

The Snowman
Raymond Briggs (author/illustrator)
Hamish Hamilton (hb) Puffin (pb)

3½ to 5

A small boy unable to sleep is amazed when looking out of the window to see that the snowman he has made the previous day has now come alive. Invited into the house, the snowman plays with the lights, taps and gas stove before going upstairs and fooling around in the bedroom occupied by the boy's parents, now both fast asleep. The two friends then have a meal before going outside and flying hand in hand together in the moonlit, snowy night. Passing over Brighton and then the Sussex Downs (where the author-artist lives himself), they finally part affectionately as morning approaches. But when the boy wakes up later on and rushes out to see his new friend again, all he finds is a small heap of melting snow.

First published in 1978 and a bestseller ever since, this story of friendship and final loss has captivated audiences both as a book and later as an animated film. Although the events within it take place in winter, it has

3¹/₂ to 5

an appeal which lasts all year round. The idea of a perfect imaginary friend known only to the child is always a popular one, and it is made more so here by the unpredictable and continuously entertaining way in which the snowman alternates between behaving like a small child and an all-powerful adult. Child readers can therefore both love this amiable night visitor and find themselves joining in the occasional scolding he receives when he goes too far and has to be rescued by the boy himself. Yet on the whole the mood here is one of affection for someone who, despite faults often shared by children themselves,

remains a true friend from first to last. The final moment when he melts away, is not really sad because every child knows that snow never lasts anyway. But it does represent a coming-to-terms with change in a way that even small children can readily understand as well as accept. There is also all the fun of seeing an impossible dream realized with such brilliance, illustrative power and deep underlying sympathy. Told in a series of pictures – some small and comic-strip style, others full-page – this complex and technically innovative story is made easy to follow because of the interest and empathy it inspires in readers of any age.

Something Else
Kathryn Cave (author) **Chris Riddell** (illustrator)
Puffin (pb)

The fantastical little hero of this story looks a bit like a cross between a human and koala bear, but although he tries to join in with the community of talking rabbits, storks, giraffes and others living around him, somehow he never quite fits in – hence his name, "Something Else". But one day another odd creature arrives at his door, and after initially sending him away Something Else changes his mind, realizing that he can still be friends even with someone so unlike himself. The two friends play happily together before finally welcoming into their home yet another Something Else – in this case, an ordinary human child.

Infants with some experience of life outside the home may well recognize the situation described in this book, where whatever they do in the company of others never

3¹/₂ to 5

seems to be quite right. As in this story, there
are days at
school
when a
game
proves
too
difficult, a
painting is
held up to
ridicule and
even
opening
a
packed
lunch
turns into a

social disaster. By showing that these experiences are
common to everyone, the story suggests that while
others should try to be tolerant of individuals it's also
important for those same individuals to be tolerant as
well. This could sound rather like a sermon, but Chris
Riddell's joyful illustrations make this a book to enjoy
as well as to ponder over. His depiction of Something
Else's patched-up furniture suggests all the comfortable
warmth of a familiar home, and the pictures of the
various animals at play make them look extremely
human at the same time.

Stellaluna

Janell Cannon (author/illustrator)

David Bennett Books (pb)

First published in America, this picture book about a small bat has illustrations that combine accurate observation with a magical, luminous atmosphere. It tells the story of Stellaluna, a baby fruit bat who gets separated from her mother when they are both attacked by an owl. Ending up with a family of birds, she learns to adopt their ways, with predictable mishaps when she tries to fly during the day. Reunited with her mother again, she re-learns the ways of bats and, in doing so, teaches young readers something about these fascinating creatures. The story ends with a two-page appendix above the heads of small readers, providing rather terse information about various bat matters such as echolocation, pollination and the regeneration of tropical forests. But children will thrill to the story, with its powerful illustrations and touching story. While so many animal stories opt for basically human situations, this one gets much closer to nature in a way that a child can both understand and enjoy.

The Story of Babar: the Little Elephant

Jean de Brunhoff (author/illustrator)

Random House (hb)

3½ to 5

First written in the form of illustrated letters to his children when the author was separated from them by illness, this classic story was published in 1934 and has remained a favourite ever since. Starting with Babar's birth and ending with his marriage – where he and Celeste fly away from their wedding feast in a glorious yellow balloon – the story has the sweep, conviction and occasional hint of sadness found in the very best fairy tales. Having lost his mother early on to a "cruel hunter", Babar runs away to a typical small French town where he is befriended by a kindly (as well as very rich) old lady. A shopping trip ensues, made famous by his delight in going up and down in the lift before being warned off by the lift-boy with the words: "Sir, this is not a toy. You must get out now and buy what you want." Finally returning home to take up the vacant crown, King Babar always remains something of a child to the last.

3¹/₂ to 5

This picture book broke many of the conventional publishing rules of its time, appearing in a large format and with a hand-written text. Even today, in a smaller size and using ordinary print, it still feels both fresh and original. Its generous use of white space means that significant details have a chance to stand out and be noticed rather than being swamped by everything else going on. The various clothes Babar buys, or the photograph taken of him – reproduced on the page to look like an actual portrait – make an immediate impression. At other times, a full-page spread aimed at establishing an overall atmosphere leaves readers with the enjoyable task of picking out all the many details for themselves. When Babar goes out for a jaunt in his little red sports car, an object of acute longing for generations of children who have read this story, the surrounding countryside teems with life: on the river, barges are decked with washing hung out to dry while anglers, swimmers and a passing train make up the rest of the background. When Babar weeps, his whole body droops with sadness. At other times he is urbane sophistication personified, lecturing friends of the old lady about life in the Great Forest while clothed in evening dress and leaning nonchalantly on one elbow.

This story has sometimes been criticized as justifying a type of colonialism, with Babar portrayed as the native prince who comes back to rule after receiving his education and values in the West. But for generations of children, it is simply a story about growing up and becoming independent. First seen riding on his mother's back, Babar eventually develops into a competent young man, popular with everyone, good at his lessons and an excellent guide to his two little elephant cousins who come up to town to bring him home. Leaving behind his staunch friend the old lady is a second and final separation from the dependency he has felt up to that moment; after that he can take up a fully adult role at home while at the same time choosing an attractive young wife. Young readers still far from independent themselves can get a taste of maturity from this story while also enjoying all the different adventures, meals, purchases and journeys that occur along the way. Other Babar books exist, including a number devised by the author's son Laurent, but none are as fine as this, which remains one of the outstanding books written for children during the last century.

The Tale of Peter Rabbit

Beatrix Potter (author/illustrator)
Frederick Warne (hb & pb)

No better illustrated story for small children has ever been created than this one, which began as a letter

Beatrix Potter sent to a friend's child in 1893. With little space to spare on the page, this first account of Peter Rabbit was written with a brisk economy of words, interspersing pictures wherever there was room. When she came to design a book from her original idea several years later, she insisted that it remain a size small enough for an infants' grasp. The finished book, first published in

3½ to 5

1902, maintained the same direct quality in its prose, with small illustrations adding extra detail. Almost immediately it became a children's classic and has remained popular with young readers ever since.

Although she had no children of her own, Beatrix Potter enjoyed many friendships with the young and seemed to know better than any other author-illustrator at the time what exactly they were looking for in their stories. Small children enjoy the idea of mischievousness, for example, and Peter Rabbit is a natural rebel. But children also have a strong sense of justice, so that when Peter falls sick at the end of his story they readily understand that he has brought it on himself. Before that, Peter escapes death by inches on several occasions as he runs from the fearsome and aggrieved Mr McGregor whose garden he has been raiding. At other times, Peter weeps when things seem really hopeless, only to bound back at the very last moment. This struggle to survive is no joke for Peter, and his predicament is something that children take seriously.

While other books at this age present a softened view of life, Beatrix Potter – befitting someone who was also a practical Lake District farmer – did not believe in sentimentality when writing for the young. Like the fairy tales she so admired, she preferred stories that often included real danger as well as last-minute rescues. That this was an inspired approach is demonstrated by the intense interest children have always shown in her stories. It is rare to see a small child laughing at Peter Rabbit and his adventures. It is equally rare to see infants bored by him; what is going on in this story is far too important to them for that.

The illustrations show Peter starting off as a rather humanized creature, with powers of speech and wearing his famous blue coat, but he ends up looking much more like a wild animal, having mislaid his clothes in addition to almost losing his life. It is typical of an artist who never believed in giving young readers too much at a time, that her pictures often contain subtle but effective details – such as the time that Peter hides in a watering can, his presence indicated only by his long ears sticking out of its top. Less of the beautiful Lakeland scenery appears in this story than in some of the other books, but even so the mood – as in many of her stories – is one of background tranquillity in contrast to the drama of the actual plot.

Beatrix Potter wrote and illustrated twenty-three books for children, and while a few are of variable quality the best remain in a class of their own. They also have the additional advantage of appearing in a uniform series excellent for collecting, with characters from various different stories regularly appearing on the back covers or inside the pages of each other's books. To celebrate the centenary of the first publication of *The Tale of Peter Rabbit*, Frederick Warne

3½ to 5

have brought out an especially handsome new edition with six additional original illustrations – two of which have never before been printed, and four which were dropped for the 1904 edition.

Some Favourite Beatrix Potter Titles

The Tale of Squirrel Nutkin

The Tailor of Gloucester

The Tale of Benjamin Bunny

The Tale of Two Bad Mice

The Tale of Mrs. Tiggy-Winkle

The Tale of Mr. Jeremy Fisher

The Tale of Tom Kitten

The Tale of Jemima Puddle-Duck

The Tale of The Flopsy Bunnies

The Tale of Mrs. Tittlemouse

The Tale of Pigling Bland

The Tale of Samuel Whiskers

The Tale of Little Pig Robinson

Thomas the Tank Engine

Rev. W. Awdry (author)

Heinemann (hb)

Thomas is a cheeky little steam engine who has many adventures with his other engine friends Gordon, Edward, Henry, James plus various others. They all live on the imaginary Island of Sodor, which resembles an idealized rural Britain at a time in the past when important functionaries – like the Fat Controller who regularly features in these stories – still wore top hats. Gender distinctions are equally old-fashioned, with all the engines shown as strongly masculine, while the female coaches and trucks are portrayed as silly, noisy and complaining. Each short story ends on a strong moral note, with boastful engines always sure to receive their comeuppance while modest heroics are eventually rewarded.

Originally told to his three-year-old son Christopher when recovering from an attack of measles, these stories, although completely imaginary, also reflect the author's lifetime love affair with everything to do with steam engines. Details of various railway equipment and industrial practices are often wholly accurate, and the author was particularly keen that accompanying illustrations stuck as closely as possible to the technical specifications laid down by him. This attention to detail cut both ways, though, with numbers of young readers sometimes spotting tiny inconsistencies before showering the author with letters gleefully pointing out the mistakes.

It would have been impossible to guess at the enormous popularity that the books were to enjoy when this first title appeared in 1946. But children, especially boys, have always been fascinated by trains, and these

3½ to 5

little books, which are easy to hold, offered them engines galore. When merchandizing eventually arrived in the form of toys, clothes and even whole model railway systems, Thomas and his friends became even more famous. Video and theatrical adaptations followed, but the books themselves continue to sell in vast numbers. The world they portray, although serene and secure, has enough minor accidents going on to maintain a certain level of suspense. The strong sense of family binding the engines together also has its attractions, as does the regular pattern of each story where minor faults are first identified and then usually forgiven by the end. This firmly moralistic approach is balanced by the sheer delight the author takes in the engines themselves, from their gleaming paintwork to their selfless courage when the going gets really tough. Chattering to each other like children, they make for bright and mostly cheerful characters – with the additional advantage of being inspired by the golden age of steam when the romance of rail travel was at its height.

Awdry and his Illustrators

C. Reginald Dalby, the man responsible for giving Thomas the Tank Engine his original form, didn't really care for trains, and despite his lively characterization of Thomas and the other engines, his relaxed attitude to detail drew a steady stream of letters from young readers eager to point out his mistakes. Following an argument with the Rev. W. Awdry in 1956, Dalby declined to continue with the Railway Series and the following year his place was taken by **John T. Kenney**. Kenney, himself a train enthusiast, got on with Awdry much better and his depictions of the railway are both more realistic and less toy-like. Just five years and six titles later, though, he was forced to retire by failing eyesight. Determined to carry on, the publishers approached a younger artist, **Gunvor Edwards**, to see if she would continue the series. In the end it was her husband, **Peter Edwards**, who did much of the draughtsmanship and he went on to illustrate a further eight titles, culminating in 1972 with the twenty-sixth, *Tramway Engines* – the very last book to be authored by Awdry.

3¹/₂ to 5

The Tiger Who Came to Tea

Judith Kerr (author/illustrator)

HarperCollins (hb & pb)

3¹/₂ to 5

Sophie is sitting down to eat with her mother when a big furry tiger rings the doorbell and invites himself to tea. Beaming from ear to ear, he proceeds to eat everything there is and then drinks all the water in the tap. It's not until he has politely taken his leave that Sophie and her mother realize there is nothing left for Daddy to eat when he comes home. The problem is solved by a pleasant family meal in a nearby café, and although Sophie buys a very big tin of Tiger Food in case of any more visits, their unexpected visitor is never seen again.

The very idea of a huge tiger coming to tea could seem rather frightening, but all such worries are immediately

banished in this artful little book. It is clear from his
first entrance that Sophie adores this tiger, gazing
admiringly at his tail and later hugging him as well as
taking a ride on his back. He is far more a friendly
outsize ginger cat than a wild animal, with Katie and
her mother treating him with the affection normally
reserved for a favourite pet. The home life the tiger
shares for a while is shown as close and loving, with
smiles all round as the little family takes itself off for a
meal of sausages, chips and ice cream. First written and
illustrated in 1968, this remains an irresistible book,
whose pictures of London streets thronged with little
shops with no cars parked outside add a note of
pleasant nostalgia for older readers as well.

Where's Wally?
Martin Handford (illustrator)
Walker Books (pb)

This is a quite extraordinary book,
practically ageless in its appeal and
superb for passing great swathes of
time with no risk of boredom. Wally
himself is a somewhat nerdy traveller
who is about to set off for a
worldwide hike, complete with
glasses, sensible shoes and a stout

3½ to 5

walking stick. Readers can follow his progress through beaches and ski slopes to safari parks and fun fairs – but only if they are able to find him first. For on each large two-page spread detailing Wally's progress, his distinctive presence is masked by the addition of hundreds of other people, all doing their own thing. The challenge is not just to spot Wally himself in each picture, but also to find his dog (visible only by its tail), his key, a camera, a scroll and a pair of binoculars plus a host of other characters.

Searching for obscure objects hidden amidst so much detail could become tedious, but Mark Handford maintains interest throughout by adding numbers of excellent visual puns as well. His airport scene, for example, includes a fork-lift truck carrying an enormous domestic fork, while beneath a windsock he inserts a huge slipper. Humour elsewhere is broad enough for even the simplest of tastes, with people bumping into each other, falling over, getting squirted by hosepipes and providing targets for a little boy's catapult. The final page contains checklists for extra details on each page that might not have been spotted before, but there are no clues for finding Wally – that is something all readers must do for themselves. Given that he always wears the same clothes – a striped pullover, bobble hat and jeans – it's not too difficult a task, although very small readers might have to work hard. In doing so they will also be learning how to organize their own powers of perception most efficiently when it comes to making a visual search, a skill that could well prove useful once in school. This exuberant and continuously inventive book and its various sequels have now sold over thirty million copies in more than twenty countries, and it is easy to see why.

Wombat Goes Walkabout
Michael Morpurgo (author) **Christian Birmingham** (illustrator)
HarperCollins (hb & pb)

A young wombat gets lost in the Australian outback. He sets out to find his mother, but the other creatures he meets along the way make fun of him when he tells them that all he can do is dig and think. But these two abilities save them when a bush fire breaks out and they all need somewhere to shelter. The story ends with the wombat reunited with his mother and enjoying new respect from those who formerly mocked him.

Any story involving the search for a mother who is temporarily lost stands a good chance of capturing young readers' attention from the start. But this book also has the added appeal of its extraordinary illustrations. The artist knows Australia well, and the glowing pictures of exotic scenery that result are truly special. The wildlife shown in these illustrations will be largely unfamiliar to infants living in Britain, and all the more fascinating for that. Picture books were once potent instruments for broadening the minds of the young as well as enriching their imagination. TV now has the primary role when it comes to providing pictures of wildlife, but books still have much to offer and a picture book can be returned to over and over again, their illustrations revealing more as children grow in their powers of understanding. This is just one picture book that, while entertaining children, also teaches them something of value about the world they live in and its infinite variety.

Zagazoo
Quentin Blake (author/illustrator)
Red Fox (pb)

This ingenious picture book offers readers no less than a complete tour of the seven ages of childhood. Delivered (by post) of a dear little infant, proud parents George and Bella see their child change first into a baby vulture and then in quick succession into a small elephant, a warthog, a bad-tempered dragon, a bat and a tall, hairy creature who gets bigger by the day. Just when George and Bella – visibly ageing themselves – have almost given up, the hairy creature changes overnight into a young man with perfect manners. No more transformations occur after that, but when their son finally decides to get married himself, he finds that his parents have changed into a pair of large, brown pelicans. Readers will soon catch on to what is happening here, identifying the screams of the baby vulture or the clumsiness of the small elephant with what they recognise from their own past experience. And although George and Bella find some of the changes hard to take, the last picture shows the two, aged pelicans walking off with their son and his girl friend all showing the utmost affection for each other. The prevailing mood of this wise as well as riotous picture book is always more of wonder than of any lingering child or parental resentment. As the author-illustrator writes himself on the last page, "Isn't life amazing!"

3½ to 5

231

Poetry

Poems for this age group can afford to be longer than before, sometimes telling a definite story on the way. Like small children, they are not always particularly well-behaved in themselves, and are occasionally written in the same spirit found in playground chants and teases. A few of the following poems might run the risk of offending some adults because of their sense of mischief. But children often enjoy these most of all, relishing the chance to join in verses reflecting the more unruly sides of their own imagination.

Other equally popular poems for this age group concentrate on gentler feelings, or else branch out into a nonsense world full of charming impossibilities. British writers have always shown a particular talent for creating attractive nonsense, often stretching children's imagination to the limits in the process. Children in their turn have a capacity for appreciating both everyday reality and wild fantasy in the pictures and stories they like, as well as in the imaginative games they most enjoy playing. During such games, for example, an ordinary object such as a pencil can, if necessary, be instantly transformed into a pistol, an aeroplane or almost anything else required. In the same way, tables can become tents while upturned stools may serve as boats. Poetry has always recognised this ability children have to imagine the possible and the impossible almost at the same moment. Putting such feelings into rhyme gives them back to children in a form that at its best has always proved immensely pleasurable, often lending itself to near-instant memorization at the same time.

The Cat in the Hat

Dr Seuss (author/illustrator)

HarperCollins (hb & pb)

Dr Seuss, the assumed name of Ted Giesel, was an American advertising man who brought all his skills as a cartoonist and copywriter into his many books for the young. His unstuffy if unsubtle sense of humour proved instantly popular, particularly with smaller children who relished his firm sense of rhythm and rhyme. The universe he creates is at times surreal in its complete separation from the ordinary and everyday.

Using the minimum of a few simple words in a parody of an old-fashioned early Reading Primer, his first early learning "Beginner Book" *The Cat in the Hat* opened up a new world of children's humour when it appeared in 1957. Two children feeling bored and left on their own during a rainy day receive a visit from a flamboyant cat dressed in a red bow-tie, a large hat and nothing else. He suggests some excellent games but these also have the unfortunate effect of creating a lot of mess. Things get worse when he introduces his two friends, Thing One and Thing Two – typical Seuss half-animal, half-human cartoon creations. With mother about to return the situation is critical, but everything is resolved when the Cat shows an unexpected ability to clear up, leaving the house as spotless as when he arrived.

This story, told in the easiest of rhymes, offers young readers an ingenious combination of order and mayhem. While the cat is altogether too wild, the family goldfish, who constantly warns the two children against him, is rather too law-abiding. Children themselves, aware of both such conditions within themselves, can both revel with the Cat and then side with the Goldfish when it looks as if everyone is going to get into deep trouble. Accompanying pictures make the same point, with the Cat forever appearing the complete, supremely confident showman and the two children always looking rather apprehensive. Over and above all this, there is a restless energy, constantly pushing the story to new imaginative excesses while filling each illustration with the visual equivalent of a firework display. Reading

Primers found in schools at the time were usually dull and lifeless but after publication of this book, the existence of a limited vocabulary could never again be used as an excuse for writing a boring, pointless story. Dr Seuss showed that simple language is no handicap to producing outsize tales, particularly when they are illustrated with the type of over-the-top verve always to be associated with his name. If your child enjoys this, *The Cat in the Hat Comes Back* is more in the same vein.

3¹/₂ to 5

Cats Sleep Anywhere
Eleanor Farjeon (author) **Anne Mortimer** (illustrator)
Frances Lincoln (hb & pb)

Eleanor Farjeon wrote many poems for children, but
this short verse has always been a particular favourite.
In this edition it is magically illustrated by Anne
Mortimer, with each page lingering on one more
picture of a cat sound asleep. Whether they're on "Any
table, / Any chair, / Top of piano, / Window-ledge, / In
the middle, / On the edge", all the different cats on
show here display the same look of total concentration
– even when sleeping in incongruous places such as an
empty shoe or on top of an occupied dog kennel.
Almost real enough to stroke, they will surely please
many older readers as well as the smaller children for
whom this book is primarily intended.

Green Eggs and Ham
Dr Seuss (author/illustrator)
HarperCollins (hb & pb)

In *Green Eggs and Ham* the author-artist's illustrations
of grotesque creatures again burst into life with an
energy that at times almost threatens to leap off the
page. Trains and cars also go airborne in sheer
exhilaration, with speed indicated by the type of visual

exclamation marks common in comic strip art. Railway
lines are held up by twisted branches of wood,
themselves perched perilously on the spikes of a red
mountain. And in the determination of the central

character,
"Sam-I-Am", to
find a taker for
his dish of
green eggs and
ham, he
invokes a series
of crazed
pictorial
images all
taken from
simple rhymes
such as boat
and goat or
box and fox.
Some children
have learned to
read mainly

from Dr Seuss's many publications, given that his texts
are often so memorable as well as visually entertaining.
Others simply enjoy the rollercoaster ride offered here
and elsewhere by an author-artist who was without
doubt something of a genius.

I Saw Esau

Iona and Peter Opie (editors) **Maurice Sendak** (illustrator)

Walker Books (pb)

3¹/₂ to 5

This collection features numbers of the sort of
traditional rhymes known to children over centuries
but usually thought too raw to get into more
respectable nursery rhyme anthologies. They combine
clever rhymes, tongue-twisters, and riddles, all of the
type that can gain children popularity once rattled off
in front of others of the same age, such as that
distressing saga starting "Quick! Quick! / The cat's been
sick." There is also a selection of stinging replies useful
for repelling verbal attacks from others and plenty of
tricks, such as: "Adam and Eve and Pinch-me / Went
down to the river to bathe; / Adam and Eve were
drowned, / Who d'you think was saved?" Has there ever
been a child who has not fallen for this one? Other
rhymes accompany games of skipping, make fun of
school or play upon the secrets that children often feel
the need to keep.

This particular edition also has the advantage of
scholarly notes at the back of the book from the two
folklorist-editors plus illustrations by the incomparable
Maurice Sendak. These range from funny to the darkly
mysterious, sometimes linking two quite diverse
rhymes into one picture. They are not always for the
squeamish – one series of tiny illustrations shows a

baby actually eating its own mother. These accompany a well-known verbal trick whereby a child is requested to start off with "I one my mother, I two my mother" and so on until the unwary victim finds they are actually saying "I eight my mother". But this still comes over as good, make-believe fun – albeit of the verbally aggressive type enjoyed by so many children when among friends. But other pictures are perfectly innocent, as well as often very funny too. The rather plain, squashed-looking children this artist creates always seem to come out winners in the end, making this unique collection thoroughly friendly in atmosphere. Adults who feel less enthusiastic about some of it should perhaps ask themselves whether they have forgotten the sort of thing they once used to say and do in the playground.

The Quangle Wangle's Hat
Edward Lear (author) **Helen Oxenbury** (illustrator)
Mammoth (pb)

This mysterious magical poem by Edward Lear is brought to life here by one of Britain's top illustrators in a way few readers will forget. Starting with the Quangle Wangle himself, whose actual face is never seen, the rest of this picture book describes all the different animals who are given permission to build their nest in his hundred-and-two-foot-wide hat. These include famous characters from other Lear poems such as "The Pobble Who Has No Toes" and "The Dong with a Luminous Nose". Both emerge as entirely credible creations, intricately coloured, full of movement and with every expectation that they will provide excellent company for future neighbours like "The blue Baboon who played the flute, / And the Orient Calf from the Land of Tute." Lear's own drawings for his poems were in pen-and-ink, but these illustrations, with their swirling colours, varied shapes and packed detail, are more user-friendly for small children. Helen Oxenbury is an artist on her own, highly original and with an extraordinary ability to share the affection she so obviously feels for her creations.

Revolting Rhymes
Roald Dahl (author) **Quentin Blake** (illustrator)
Puffin (pb)

This collection features six well-known fairy tales as they've not been heard before, told in verse that never lets a bad rhyme get in the way of overall dash and energy. One quotation, taken from "Little Red Riding Hood and the Wolf" at the moment when our heroine is about to be devoured, illustrates what readers can expect: "The small girl smiles. One eyelid flickers. / She whips a pistol from her knickers. / She aims it at the creature's head / And *bang, bang, bang*, she shoots him dead." Little Red Riding Hood gets a "lovely furry wolfskin coat" into the bargain, later to be joined by a smart pigskin travelling case after she takes an equally ruthless

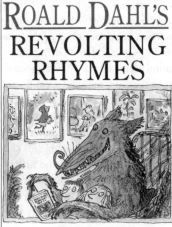

ROALD DAHL'S
REVOLTING
RHYMES

with illustrations by
QUENTIN BLAKE

line with the last of the three little pigs.

Some parents may not be overjoyed by verse like this, which also includes throwaway references to bowels, disastrous personal hygiene, dog dirt and various other unconventional sources for humour in children's literature. But young readers will probably love it all, given that Dahl has an uncanny way of replicating the way in which they like talking and joking among themselves – particularly when no adults are around to curb possible excesses. The deep vein of comic cynicism in these rhymes could also come as a relief to small children who may up to this moment have had little

3½ to 5

experience of literature so defiantly not on its best behaviour. But violence, vulgarity and vengefulness have an important place in the human imagination, and it is no accident that Dahl has always been immensely popular with the young. He has the ability to make every moment seem funny as well as subversive, but all this would count for nothing were he not also such a skilled writer, as this mock-savage (but really quite affectionate) book of verses demonstrates. Although not really suitable for children at the younger end of this age group – who may not recognize the fairy stories being sent up anyway – this is a book that other readers including parents will probably find themselves laughing over every time.

When We Were Very Young
A.A.Milne (author) **Ernest Shepard** (illustrator)
Methuen (hb & pb)

First published in 1924 and reprinted innumerable times since, this famous book of verse drew its inspiration not just from observations of the author's child Christopher Robin but also from his own happy childhood memories. Although the settings for these poems have dated, with their casual references to nannies, old currency and obscure bits of children's clothing, their psychological understanding is timeless.

Every mood is covered, from the simple joy of being alive ("Christopher Robin goes hoppity, hoppity") to other more reflective moments of the type found in "Halfway down the stairs." Ernest Shepard's illustrations perfectly catch this mixture of moods, suggesting that play – and indeed the whole world of a child's imagination – can be a serious as well as a potentially joyous place within which to explore.

By no means all these poems concern Christopher Robin. There is also an glimpse of Pooh in "Teddy Bear", the infectiously rhythmical "James James Morrison Morrison Weatherby George Dupree" and the famous saga of "The King's Breakfast", still one of the best-known children's poems in the language. The book ends with "Vespers", also once extremely popular but more often parodied today than heard in its original

3½ to 5

form. But like the street traders, nursery chairs and top-hatted doctors also featured in these verses, such glimpses of an age now lost can sometimes have an extra fascination of their own simply because they are no longer common currency today. One of the particular gifts older books have always offered children is a break from the present coupled with a realization that other times once existed when things could sometimes be very different. Milne was so pleased with Shepard's illustrations that he took the unusual step of making sure that the artist always had a share of the huge royalties that his books went on to earn.

Index

D

E

F

Index

Index

Y

Z

Index